"Habib captures the real struggles of survival and adaptation into a new world and its adversities—a world that puts Africa and its people in one box. Like the author, I come from an African country, but my black skin rarely became visible until I crossed continents and arrived in the US. I highly recommend this book. It brings an addition to the American immigrant story that we need to read about."
—Abdi Nor Iftin, author of *Call Me American*

"Habib Fanny's honest and moving memoir is a fascinating saga of escape and discovery. With shining intelligence as a guidestar and reason as a compass, he navigates the turbulent waters of immigration and cultural diversity without losing his wits or his wit."
—Dan Barker, author of *Godless: How An Evangelical Preacher Became One of America's Leading Atheists*

"With humility and humor, Habib takes us on his personal adventure in this engaging and clever memoir. *A Gazelle Ate My Homework* is a captivating look into what it means to be an immigrant, an apostate, and finally, an American."
—David Consiglio, Jr., author of *Spoiler Alert: Everyone Dies*™, educator, and advocate

"Read Habib's book for the humor, but mostly for the wisdom. Read it because reading his writing is fun, but mostly because it's insightful. Read this book because it will change the way you see the world, but mostly because it will change you."
—Dushka Zapata, author of *How To Be Ferociously Happy*

"Habib Fanny's observations are thoughtful, witty, and inciteful without being cruel, which makes him a unicorn in the area of social commentary."
—Mercedes R. Lackey, author of the Heralds of Valdemar series

A Gazelle Ate My Homework

A GAZELLE ATE MY HOMEWORK

A Journey from Ivory Coast to America,
from African to Black, and from
Undocumented to Doctor

(With Side Trips into Several
Religions and Assorted
Misadventures)

Habib Fanny

with a foreword by Ali A. Rizvi

Thorntree  Press

A Gazelle Ate My Homework
A Journey from Ivory Coast to America, from African to Black, and from Undocumented to
Doctor (With Side Trips into Several Religions and Assorted Misadventures)

Thorntree Press, LLC
P.O. Box 301231
Portland, OR 97294
press@thorntreepress.com

Thorntree Press's activities take place on traditional and ancestral lands of the Coast Salish
people, including the Chinook, Musqueam, Squamish and Tsleil-Waututh nations.

Cover art: *Uit de dierenwereld*, De Ruyter & Meijer, 1873 / Rijksmuseum
Cover design by Hardest Walk
Interior illustrations from Plate 100: Antilopina, *Kunstformen der Natur* by Ernst Haeckel,
1904, public domain.
Photo on p. 168 © Ashley Ward
Interior design by Jeff Werner
Substantive editing by Andrea Zanin
Copy-editing by Hazel Boydell
Proofreading by Heather van der Hoop

Library of Congress Cataloging-in-Publication Data
Names: Fanny, Habib, 1986- author.
Title: A gazelle ate my homework : a journey from Ivory Coast to America, from African
to black, and from undocumented to doctor (with side trips into several religions and
assorted misadventures) / Habib Fanny.
Description: Portland, OR : Thorntree Press, [2020] | Summary: "From a childhood in Ivory
Coast to a career as an American physician, Habib Fanny journeys across continents, cultures and
identities, telling a few tall tales and finding his own story along the way"-- Provided by publisher.
Identifiers: LCCN 2019032944 (print) | LCCN 2019032945 (ebook) | ISBN 9781944934941
(paperback) | ISBN 9781944934958 (ebook) | ISBN 9781944934965 (kindle edition) | ISBN
9781944934972 (pdf)
Subjects: LCSH: Fanny, Habib, 1986- | Physicians--United States--Biography. | African
American physicians--United States--Biography. | Ivoirians--United States--Biography.
Classification: LCC R154.F35 A3 2020 (print) | LCC R154.F35 (ebook) | DDC 610.92 [B]--dc23
LC record available at https://lccn.loc.gov/2019032944
LC ebook record available at https://lccn.loc.gov/2019032945

10 9 8 7 6 5 4 3 2 1

Printed in the United States of America on sustainably sourced paper.

MIX
Paper from
responsible sources
FSC
www.fsc.org   FSC® C011935

To my nieces and nephews,
who fill my heart with joy.

*Am I then more of an American than
those who drew their first breath
on American Ground?*

—Alexander Hamilton

Contents

Acknowledgments

Above all, I am forever indebted to my mother, Amy Diallo, who took a huge gamble by selling all her possessions and moving us to the US, thereby making this story possible.

I am also thankful for the help of our immigration lawyer, Charles Owen, whose tireless efforts and amiability were indispensable in helping us win our case for asylum.

Of the many teachers at my high school who helped me well beyond what they were required to do, I am especially grateful to Mignon Hayes, Sandra Hagman, and Cindy Blanchard-Kronig.

Dave Consiglio started out as one of those teachers, but has now morphed into an amalgam of friend, mentor, and tormentor. He has been there, supporting me in all my endeavors for half my life, and I can never thank him enough.

Meeting June Swartz, my college counselor, was one of the best things to ever happen to me. I would not have been able to afford college without her assistance.

I am beholden to my alma mater, Eastern Michigan University, and especially to Cynthia Van Pelt and Bernice Lindke for their timely assistance in the form of grants and scholarships.

I am also much obliged to the community of readers, fellow nerds, and friends I found on Quora, without whom this book would never have been envisaged.

Turning the germ of an idea into a finished manu-script was more challenging than I could have imagined, and I owe many words of gratitude to Andrea Zanin and Hazel Boydell for their editorial assistance.

Merci beaucoup.

Foreword

Habib Fanny is many things at once. He lives in many places at once. And that's why his book isn't just one to be read, but experienced.

One minute, he's walking you through the streets of Abidjan, his hometown in the Ivory Coast—a child playing soccer with his cousins and greeting passersby in French. The next, you're with him as he does his rounds in a Michigan hospital, where his soon-to-be-mortified patient mistakes him for kitchen staff. He is a writer and a doctor, and has been a nurse. He is Ivorian and American. He is a former Muslim who briefly became Christian before becoming an agnostic and later an atheist. He is both an African in America, and an African American.

Although Habib and I come from completely different backgrounds, we are more alike than different. I am a Pakistani-born Canadian whose parents migrated from India during the 1947 partition. Like Habib, I am a writer and a physician. Like him, I am a former Muslim who is now an atheist. And like him, I am an introvert who often feels like an outsider. We live in a time where so many are focused on their identity—rediscovering it, holding on to it, finding pride and purpose in it—yet Habib and I have repeatedly shed our identities, reached beyond them, and built new ones.

While we value diversity—after all, a world that values diversity is what made our stories possible—we also understand that diversity isn't just about people who look different but think alike. In this book, you will feel the tensions between African immigrants in America and African Americans who have lived here for generations. You'll understand that Muslims are no different from any other religious community. Just as there are lapsed Catholics, secular Jews, and ex-Mormons, there are countless young Muslims who have left the faith of their parents and embraced secular, Enlightenment values. You'll learn why some immigrants to the United States, who put everything on the line to come here, appreciate and revere the rights and freedoms of their adopted home much more than some of those born and raised here, who often take them for granted. Your understanding of patriotism, group identity, and diversity itself—the topics that are central to much of our discourse today—will be challenged and turned on their heads.

What is identity? Is it the cards we're dealt at birth—the race, nationality, sexual orientation, or even religion that we identify with? Is it the life we build, the fruits of our self-directed work that indelibly become a part of us? Or is it both? And how much does it really matter? Can we be liberated from having a rigid sense of identity? Might that allow us to cling less to our biases, open ourselves up, and let the world shape us instead of us shaping the world through our identity-clouded lenses?

And what do we mean by progress, growth, evolution? Is it about taking pride in birth identities and traditions that we did not work to earn? Or is about reaching beyond our birth identities and aspiring to something bigger?

The thing about children who grew up in different cultures—third culture kids, as they're called—is that we are fundamentally incapable of seeing the world from just one perspective. Habib can effortlessly relate to children from the streets of West Africa. He understands the prejudices faced by African Americans burdened with a dark legacy of slavery and oppression. He can converse about the impacts of colonialism in fluent French and seamlessly schmooze with the elite physician community in the United States as one of them. To do all of these things, he only needs to be himself. None of these aspects of his identity are contrived.

Third culture kids naturally have a high threshold for being offended. In our current outrage culture, where a single tweet can get you "canceled," this quality is invaluable. When Habib's patient mistakes him for kitchen staff because of his skin color, he understands that the man is likely a "victim of the kind of prejudices we are all susceptible to," even questioning if he may have made the same mistake himself. When, as a new, teenage immigrant, he faces condescension and ostracism from African Americans, he doesn't write them off. Instead, it triggers his own exploration into what it means to be Black in America versus Black in Africa, leading him to question whether there really is such a thing as a singular Black culture. For Habib, adversity is never a tool of victimization. Nearly always, he turns it into an opportunity for learning and personal growth.

Like Habib himself, this book can be read and enjoyed at any level. If you're looking for a fun beach read, the lighthearted and humorous storytelling will keep you hooked. If you want a memoir that is relatable at any stratum of universal human experience, you will feel humbled and understood as Habib talks about his personal struggles with a rare kind of honesty and vulnerability that would otherwise make most of us uncomfortable. If you are looking for nuanced, meaningful social and political commentary, you will find fresh perspectives here.

The immigrant's story *is* the American story. And Habib Fanny is going to tell you his—with compassion, with empathy, and without apology.

—Ali A. Rizvi, MD
Author of *The Atheist Muslim: A Journey from Religion to Reason*

Introduction

"Every time I wake up, I see your black ass sneaking up on me!"

It was 6 AM and pitch-black outside, as it invariably was in those early winter mornings in the Midwest. Tired and chronically sleep-deprived, as was the norm with all my colleagues, I made myself get up, brave the bitter cold, and drive to the hospital for my morning rounds. I was a medical intern, having been out of med school for just half a year, and I was always gripped by the fear that my lack of experience would lead me to commit some gross error that would cause harm. Rounds didn't start until 9 AM, but you needed to be there very early if you wanted to have time to see the 10 or so patients assigned to you, put in the appropriate orders, and have all your notes written on time.

Perhaps it was the weight of the responsibilities, perhaps it was the fact that I hated having to wake up so early, or perhaps it was the short amount of time I had to do what seemed like an insurmountable amount of work, but the mornings of my first year of residency were very stressful for me. It was probably because of this that being greeted with the sentence above, irreverent as it was, was so cathartic. A white-haired veteran who had obviously decided that he was too old and too sick to give a damn about social niceties said it to me. He was a white man, only 60 years old but looking about 80 and suffering from chronic shortness of breath from a lifetime of smoking. His comment could have been offensive in another context, or had it been said to another Black physician with a sense of humor less twisted than my own, but at the time I was too busy sharing a hearty laugh with him to feel insulted.

The interaction had not come entirely out of the blue. I had met him a few days before, and by now we seemed almost old friends. I had grown up in West Africa, in a culture where sleep had an almost sacred quality, and people did not take kindly be being woken up unless there was a very good reason. And so, in those early days, I was almost apologetic for interrupting the sleep of my patients, sometimes long before sunrise. I tried to be as quiet as possible when entering the room of a sleeping patient. With this particular man, I decided to start auscultating him before waking him up. I got close, placed my stethoscope on his chest, and listened for about half a minute before he opened his eyes. He growled that I was sneaking up on him, and that he would catch me if I did it again. And soon enough, this became our game. I would try to be very quiet and reach his chest before he could open his eyes, and he would try to open his eyes before I got to him. After a few days of this, I entered the room one morning to find him wide awake, and it was then that he commented on my black ass sneaking up on him.

Maybe I had dropped some hints about my off-color sense of humor. Maybe he had initially not been amused at all, and finding me so close to his chest upon waking up triggered some PTSD symptoms. Or maybe he was just bold and didn't have any filter. Whatever it was, I was tickled enough that when I discharged him about a week later, the last thing I said to him was, "Well, I guess you won't have to worry about my black ass anymore." We shared another laugh, shook hands, and parted on good terms. And that was the end of our story. But in a sense, it was not the end. I've had many similarly colorful interactions with patients in the years since then, interactions impacted in some way not just by my complexion but also by my accent immediately betraying my foreign origins.

After graduating from residency in June 2018, I traveled back to my native Ivory Coast for the first time in 17 years. It was an occasion to reunite with family members I hadn't seen in half my lifetime, but also an opportunity to reflect on my improbable journey from young immigrant not yet fluent in English to physician, from illegal immigrant to adopted American, and to the complex identity forged along the way. The following story is the fruit of those reflections. Exotic as it might be, I hope you will find in it a typical American story.

CHAPTER 1

Kunta

"Hey, Kunta, ever been hunting a lion?"

It was always the same idiotic questions, addressed to "Kunta" or "Mutombo." I suppose these were the only African names that these high school students who had grown up and spent all their lives in a suburb of Detroit had ever encountered. And I was always left half confused, half irritated. In time, I would acquire enough fluency in English to reply right away. In time, I would learn to unleash the full fury of my sarcasm. In time, I would learn to weave an elaborate tale recounting how I had, in fact, grown up a half-savage and made my way to America by sheer force of will. But all that lay far in the future. For the time being, it was all I could do to sheepishly mutter:

"No. The only place you can see a lion in my country is at the zoo."

"Damn! You guys got zoos in Africa?"

I nodded. What else was there to do? I had moved to the US only a few months before. It was the opportunity of a lifetime. My mom had talked about immigrating to America before, but parents talk about a lot of things, and this had been something I had not quite dared to let myself dream about. But it had truly happened in the end. I was on American soil, and I was going to pursue my studies here. Imagine that! I thought of my friends back home, and of how envious they would be. America was perfection itself, the country where anyone could have access to justice, wealth, and fame, and where people could actually trust that the police were concerned with helping the population, rather than running a racketeering scheme on a grand scale.

This America of mine was not a country—it was an idea and an ideal of good governance. And nothing epitomized this idea more than the American suburb. For a kid who had grown up in Abidjan, where people urinated in the streets and littered with abandon, and where all manner of vendors occupied half the streets with their stalls and merchandise, suburbs seemed to be the pinnacle of human civilization. Here, the streets were clean, the grass of the perfectly manicured lawns was greener than anything I'd ever seen, and there were no street urchins to assault your windshield with dirty soapy water in the guise of washing it. Most astonishingly of all, when on a hot afternoon the traffic lights were broken at an intersection, drivers reacted as though there were stop signs, coordinating so that the flow of cars could continue uninterrupted. I compared this incredible scene to the pandemonium that would have ensued in Abidjan. Incredulous and spellbound, I thought, *wow, these people are so civilized!* I was falling in love with America. She was beautiful and charming. And everything she revealed and everything I discovered about her was proof that we were meant to be together. Every pleasant interaction became a vignette on the imaginary portrait I was slowly painting. Had I chosen a caption for it, it would have read: "America: Land of Perfection."

But now, several months into life in my new country, some blemishes were starting to appear on my portrait. And America was never more blemished than when people asked me idiotic questions about my origins. Did I have a pet lion? Would I be married if I were still living in Africa? Were there clicking sounds in my native language? Did I live in a hut? Had I really owned a computer in Africa? I wondered how they thought I had moved from Ivory Coast to Michigan. Had I not flown in a plane? Didn't that mean that there was an airport where I had lived? Didn't this imply the presence of electricity and some modicum of development? And if they were asking these questions, did I come across as some kind of brutish savage?

The worst part of it was that the people asking me these questions were usually the Black kids, the ones I'd assumed would have had the greatest interest in and knowledge of Africa. Instead—with the exception of one chemistry classmate, who it turns out was a Swahili-speaking halfrican—most of them seemed to have derived their knowledge of Africa from Discovery Channel documentaries. It was the Black kids who made fun of my name. It was the Black kids who laughed at me for my poor performance on the basketball court. And it was the Black kids who mocked my accent. I had admired Black American culture from afar. Seeing it up close, I was not a fan.

Adolescence is a difficult and trying time even in the best of circumstances. You're self-conscious. Strange things are happening to your body. You're old enough to ask the big questions about life, but not experienced enough to come up with adequate answers. You're teased mercilessly, and your every idiosyncrasy is dissected and put under the microscope by your peers. This process is worse if you're low in the social hierarchy. I was the half-fluent, skinny kid with a funny name and an accent. I was always going to be picked on. With the benefit of perspective and detachment, I can see that clearly now. But at the time, it seemed that I was on the receiving end of unearned hostility from the Black kids, and I paid them back in the same currency. This is how those kids, of whom there were so many in gym class and so few in calculus and physics, became for a time my only image of Black America. We were not off to a good start.

CHAPTER 2

Origin Story

My life in Africa was very different. We had very little food, eating only about once a week. Usually it was gazelle meat, laboriously acquired after spending days following hoofprints in the wilderness. Noticing the prints and tracking down a herd was the easy part, since every child older than seven needed to know such things in order to make it through our rite of passage. The difficulty lay in approaching the animal silently and hiding your scent to remain undetected. The other problem was that sometimes, after you had tracked your beast for a week, rubbed yourself with mud to hide your odor, stealthily made your way through the tall grass of the savanna, suddenly run at full tilt, and at last thrown your spear into the side of your gazelle, out of nowhere, perhaps out of envy, perhaps out of simple bad luck, perhaps as a result of dark magic from that old hag you had refused to share your meal with the week before, a lioness would appear.

It would not be a lion—they are too lazy to hunt. Instead, it would be a mighty, sinewy, angry, hungry lioness coming to wrest your prize away from you. If this happened and there were five or more hunters, you could keep her at bay by adopting a tight wall-of-spears formation—another skill you had to master for the rite of passage. But if there were only two or three people, you had to use a different stratagem. One person would have to quickly cut a leg off the gazelle while the others distracted the lioness with feigned attacks. Then it was time to quickly haul the leg over your shoulder and run away as fast as you could. Have you ever tried running with a spear in one hand, a lioness at your back, and the leg of a gazelle over your shoulder dripping blood all over your loincloth and legs? It is the worst thing imaginable, the absolute worst. But when your only choices are survival or starvation, you learn to do what you must.

As you might imagine, not everyone survived. But although my life was poor, nasty, and brutish, I was determined that it would not be short. And so, after years of living in the jungle, with its attendant bats and gnats and rats and feral cats, I decided that I had had enough, and that I would head for greener pastures. But where to go? I had heard of a place called America, where all the streets were paved with gold, and where the granaries were so full that everyone had more food than they knew what to do with. So, with my bare hands, and all by myself, since those knights of negativity and paragons of perfidy in the village would not help me, I built a little raft. My neighbors thought I was crazy.

"Habib, do you even think this thing will float?"

"Habib, where do you think you will go with this little thing?"

"Habib, don't you know the big water will swallow you whole?"

"Habib, even if you make it to the other side, don't you know there are white-skinned devils who will eat you alive?"

I did not heed any of it. Day after day, when I was not gazelle hunting or eating some fat bush rat, I was working on my raft. At last, after 40 days and 40 nights, it was ready. It was no ship-of-the-line. It was not even a galley, for that matter. But it looked for all the world like it would take me to my destination. And so, full of hope, though more than a little apprehensive, I made my way to the Atlantic, taking with me my most valuable possession—my spear. I figured it would come in handy when I got hungry along the way. In my village, I had been by far the best with a spear. No one could even pretend to compete. And other than those one or two fluke losses I sustained because my foot slipped in the mud just as I was about to release the spear, when had I ever been bested by anyone?

Unfortunately for me—and here I think it must have been the sorcery of that old hag again, because it had been obvious, even to the loudest of the naysayers, that my vessel was very sturdy and perfectly built—midway through my voyage, my raft capsized, and I had to swim the rest of the way. Have you ever tried swimming in the middle of the ocean with a spear in one hand while trying to use the other to get back on your capsized raft? I found this impossible, especially since every once in a while, a shark would mess with me and I'd have to bitchslap it to show it who was boss. Have you ever tried bitchslapping a shark underwater? I don't recommend it. You put all the energy you can muster into it, but there's so much water in the way that by the time your backhand reaches the shark's face, it thinks you're trying to pet it. It is absolutely infuriating. In any case, I was not able to get back on top of my raft, so I had to let it go. At some point—I don't recall exactly how—I lost my spear, too. I am fairly certain, but I will not not swear to it, that I did not drop it during an encounter with a whale when, although I was not scared at all, my body started shaking uncontrollably. It must have been muscle spasms from the cold.

In spite of all this, after several months, I at last reached the coast of America. By that time, I was the best swimmer humanity had ever known, and so it was child's play to dodge the US Coast Guard. And thus, fearless and spearless, but with my loincloth still intact, I arrived. I was on American soil. This was the land I had so long dreamed of. This was the land that would now be my home.

After being asked so many outlandish questions about Africa, this became my origin story—if the listener was kind enough to let me tell it without too many interruptions. It's perfectly believable if you ask me, but of course, there have always been naysayers. These skeptics, who believe themselves perspicacious when they are in fact mere killjoys, have sometimes been inclined to point out that since I was born in 1986, so long after colonization had thoroughly transformed the African landscape, and in a city of three million inhabitants, it is exceedingly doubtful that I would know anything more about spears than your average person born in, say, Chicago. Reluctantly, I find myself conceding that they have a point. But, then again, isn't this a pretty kickass origin story?

CHAPTER 3

The Chieftaîh

When I look back at my elementary school education, what strikes me now is how weighty some of the concepts we covered were. We learned some complex sentence diagramming with terms like *circumstantial complement of time*. We learned about the scourge of deforestation, and the toll it had taken on our environment. We learned about rural to urban migration, its consequences on the rural economy, and the strains it placed on municipal budgets. And we learned about colonization. This was the weightiest subject of them all. We learned that the Whites had come from afar to subjugate us, imposed a system of forced labor, and plundered our resources. Faced with long odds, our people fought bravely under heroic leaders, who unfortunately failed to unite their forces. One by one, they were crushed, and an unfair and illegitimate colonial administration was put in place. Finally, after several decades, a new generation of leaders, who had ironically been schooled by the Whites, fought for and obtained our independence. Such was the story we were taught—a classic tale of good and evil, with no room for even a semblance of nuance.

Among the heroes we learned about, one name in particular stuck with me: Samory Toure. His ambition was to forge a modern African state with a powerful military equipped with firearms. In this he succeeded, but his designs clashed with those of the French, who also wanted to carve out an empire for themselves in the aftermath of their disastrous war against Prussia. A long military struggle ensued. Bit by bit, Samory lost his territory until he was finally cornered and captured in 1898. He was exiled from Ivory Coast to faraway Gabon, where he died two years later. The fate of Samory was the fate of almost all of the warlords who tried to stand in the way of European conquest.

Much later, I learned of a man named Kelessery, who had fought under Samory. He became a chieftain of a confederation of 13 villages in the northwestern corner of Ivory Coast. The colonial administration in those days asked chieftains to provide children to be sent to schools built by the French to train the next generation of local administrators. These Africans, it was thought, fluent in French and owing their status to their French overlords, would prove to be loyal, if nothing else because of self-interest. But how loyal to their African heritage would such children be in the end? What if, having been indoctrinated by the Whites, they became, in effect, dark-skinned Whites? Would they pay their respects to their elders? Would they offer sacrifices to the spirits of the village? The chieftain could not be so sure, and so he resolved to send only the children of others.

And yet there was some hesitation in his resolve. What if, as a kinsman had asked him, these children being sent to be schooled by the Whites were being groomed to take over the running of the country tomorrow? How would he feel, knowing that he had elevated the children of others over his own? Wouldn't it be wise to send at least one of his own children? There was wisdom in the advice, but he could not bring himself to heed it fully. And so, rather than sending his firstborn son, who would be heir to his chieftancy, he decided that his second son, Yah, would be schooled. This event happened long before I was born, but it is the first turning point in my story. Yah became one of the first indigenous teachers in Ivory Coast, a position that brought him prestige and money. Owing everything he had to education, he saw it as his primary duty to his children to show them the importance of academics. A polygamist with three wives, Yah fathered 19 children. His eldest child was a daughter who became a pharmacist, which was extremely unusual for an African woman born in the 1930s. A son named Ibrahima became a dentist. And he in turn fathered five children, of whom I am the fourth.

I never knew my grandfather. He died of heart disease three years before I was born. I often wonder what he would think of me if he could see what I have become. His descendants have, for the most part, done rather well for themselves. And yet there was an unintended consequence of the way he reared his children—I am not fluent in Jula, my African language. He had insisted that his children speak only French at home. This served them well, since they all started school already fluent in the language, which gave them an edge over most other children at the time. But because my father feels more comfortable in French than Jula, we also grew up speaking French at home. And since I grew up in Abidjan—Ivory Coast's capital city that is home to many different ethnic groups whose only mutual language is the one left behind by the colonizer—I also spoke French in the streets. In the rare instances when I try to speak Jula, I sound like a French-accented toddler.

I roll my eyes whenever I hear of sacrificing to the spirits of the village. I am amused when I am told that I must do a ritual washing to ward off evil spirits. I am irreverently irreligious. I am, in short, one of those dark-skinned Whites my great-grandfather feared his progeny would become. And yet, it is ultimately his decision that made me who I am today.

CHAPTER 4

Early Years

My earliest memory is of Brazil. The year is 1989, and I am only three years old. I am there with my mother, my nine-year-old sister, Sally, and a maternal cousin whose name has escaped me. All that remains from the trip is a set of three images suspended in time, with most of the surrounding decor lost in a sea of blurriness. The first image is of a playground slide. There is a ball pit at the bottom, and I am looking at it longingly. The space around me is blurry. My mom is at my side, but I can't see her face. All I can see is that tantalizing ball pit, with its bright, colorful balls, in which I am forbidden to go swimming as I would like. There was no such slide in Ivory Coast, so for the remainder of my childhood, every time I saw a ball pit on TV, I would think of that summer spent in Brazil.

The second image is even more blurry. I am playing with my friend. His name is Diego. I speak French. He speaks Portuguese. Yet we somehow understand each other. Apparently, at the level spoken by toddlers, French and Portuguese are still mutually intelligible. What games are we playing? And what exactly are we talking about? It is all lost. The sound is gone from the scene, and so is his face. Only his name remains, in the full splendor of its exoticism. Diego, my erstwhile summer friend, where are you today?

The third image is the most memorable of the bunch. I am sitting at a table, my sister facing me, my mother at my side. We are eating. It's steak and fries, also known as double heaven. I like fries a lot. I *love* meat. I don't know when I acquired a taste for it, but along with my mom and my toys, it might be my favorite thing in the universe. I gulp down my portion of meat. I stare at my sister, who is using a fork and knife to cut tiny pieces off her steak, which she spends what seems like minutes chewing. My eyes widen. It seems to me that I simply must have this steak. She clearly does not understand the value of meat.

Look how she takes such small bites! Maybe that's all she needs. Maybe she just doesn't like steak like I do, which is fine, but this means that this steak should be mine. In an instant my arm flies, as fast as a cobra, grabbing the remaining piece of meat from her plate and shoving it into my mouth. I've done it! I have won! I have a large grin on my face, a living testament to my accomplishment. There are lightning bolts coming out of my sister's eyes. *Is this what a murderous intent looks like?* My sister tries to leave her side of the table and seize me. But my mom is there and holds her back, telling her to let it go.

Many have described the sweet taste of victory. They were wrong. Victory is not sweet. Victory is a juicy chunk of meat you have just stolen from your sister's plate, all the more delectable because you are sitting there chewing it right in front of her with a grin on your face, secure in the knowledge that your mother will protect you from any harm that might come your way. I was too young to have retained much else from this scene. Apart from the sense of triumph and glee that still makes me giggle with abandon every time I think back on that moment, the most fascinating aspect of looking back on that period is how young my mother was—36 years old! I'm only a few years away from that now. I wish I could talk to that younger mother of mine. I wish I could gaze into her face. I wish I could tell her about who I have become. Would she believe me? Would she be scared? Would she be proud? I will never know.

I have no memory of the remainder of the third year of my life, but I am aware of some events that were told and retold when I was growing up. I know of Sanata, my live-in nanny who taught me Jula. She got married and left us that year. She had been my main companion and her departure left me gripped by loneliness. I would cry and yell her name, calling for her to come back, but I never saw her again. Her husband infected her with AIDS and she died a few years later. In the years that followed, I slowly lost my fluency in Jula.

My father was flush with cash and was always buying new cars. When I was three, he had a Mercedes. So, every time I saw a Mercedes, I would turn to whoever was with me and ask, "That's Papa's car, isn't it?" Jula was the language I spoke at this age, but I always addressed my parents in French. My father was *Papa* and my mother was *Maman*. This is still what I call them.

I remember almost nothing of my fourth and fifth years. What I do remember vividly are the tiles in the yard. They were square, slightly smaller than an inch on each side, and they became my favorite toy. I would build elaborate structures and proudly show them to my mom, who in turn would show them to visitors. I was going to be an architect! I was about as sure of this as one could be of anything. But by my teenage years, I had changed my mind. Architecture no longer seemed so appealing, though I didn't know what I was going to do instead.

After moving to the US, it occurred to me that my father wanted me to become a physician. Parents can be very controlling and imperious in my culture. They don't consult you or take your feelings into account. They give you orders, which are meant to be obeyed, and which are readily enforced through corporal punishment. Openly challenging parental authority is not allowed. One of the few areas in which a child can exercise some autonomy is in the selection of a field of study. There will, of course, be some intense lobbying, as parents try to convince their children to choose lucrative careers. But there is a recognition that people have different aptitudes, and children are rarely forced into careers they strongly dislike. I seized this nugget of independence. I might not know what exactly I wanted to be, but I could exercise some freedom by not becoming what my father wanted me to be. I would not become a doctor.

CHAPTER 5

The Well Digger

Of all the years in my childhood, by far the most memorable was my sixth one. I have often looked back and wondered how 1992 could have been such a memorable year. Wouldn't it be just as likely that, in at least some of these memories, I was not actually six years old but arbitrarily assigned myself that age after the fact? It is definitely possible. And yet, purposely assigning myself another age in these memories feels even more arbitrary. With this in mind, let us return to that memorable year, and explore it with all the insights and biases that adult eyes can bring to bear on childhood memories.

When I was six, Ivory Coast won the African Cup of Nations—the biennial, continent-wide soccer competition. That year's event was held in Senegal, and our victory had been unexpected. Either our defense or our goalie must have been particularly solid that year, since we still hadn't conceded a single goal when we qualified for the final game against Ghana, our Eastern neighbor. It ended in a dull Ø-Ø and went to penalties. We watched nervously as neither team seemed able to pull ahead of the other. The game finally ended at 11-10, when the last Ghanaian player missed his shot. People ran into the yard to celebrate. Someone—perhaps it was my dad—pointed to a plane in the sky, saying that it was our players coming back with the cup! Of course, it couldn't have been, but the explanation seemed plausible at the time. This was the first time I knew what it felt like to have a victorious team. It seemed to me that the entire world was celebrating our victory.

Incidentally, this game and the World Cup final that followed in 1994 gave me a bit of a distorted view of soccer competition finals. Because both games ended in a draw and went to penalties, I assumed for a long time that this was the usual pattern for soccer finals. Only much later did I learn that 1994 had been the first time in World Cup history that the final had ended in a draw. From this, I gained a lifelong distrust of anecdotal data, born of a deep appreciation of how unrepresentative of the whole picture too few data points can be.

I was also six years old when I met my grandfather. It was not Yah, my father's father, who died three years before I was born. This was Toumany Diallo. His last name denotes his Fula origins, and is sometimes spelled *Jalloh* or *Jallow* in Anglophone countries, to better transcribe its pronunciation. The Fula are a traditionally nomadic and pastoralist ethnic group in West Africa. Toumany did not speak Fula, having grown up in a community that had long assimilated into the culture of its surrounding Mandinka neighbors in Guinea. I know nothing more of his roots in Guinea. He never wanted to talk about them, and to this day, no one in my family is quite sure of the name of the village where he grew up. All we know is it sounds like Koudala or Koundara or something similar. No one I know has ever been there. My mother suspected that he had once upon a time been very successful, before leaving this village and settling in Tabou, in the southwest of Ivory Coast. Had his business ventures soured? Was he running away? He never said, but she had suspicions about this too.

Toumany was later joined in Ivory Coast by a brother and a cousin, but he never wanted his children to have any contact with his family in Guinea. And so, my family tree on my mother's side stops with this man, who was born around 1912. With the sparse administration of French colonies at the time, and the illiteracy of the vast majority of the population, many people born then were only born *around* some year. No one born then had a birth certificate. Instead, people were taken as children to a local official who would estimate their age based on their appearance. This is how my grandfather was born not in but around 1912. It is said that one of Toumany's sons did not heed his advice to stay away from our nameless ancestral village. He left Ivory Coast, tracked down the village, and returned, only to die shortly after. The unspoken message is that he fell victim to witchcraft, and that the rest of us would do well to stay away.

By the time I met my grandfather, he was around 80 years old. To me, he might as well have been a thousand. He spoke no French, and I spoke no Jula. To my eyes, he was just a confused old man who happened to be my mother's father. He would get up to go for a walk, only to get lost for hours, forgetting his shoes at the mosque and wandering about town until someone in the family caught up with him. He knew only Jatu, my mom's little sister, who had stayed by his side and was his caretaker. He didn't know who my mother was, and he certainly didn't know who I was. My mom had never been particularly close to him, and he had never been a very affectionate father. Once, in a rare spell of lucidity, he spoke to her of times past. Then he started talking about his children, one by one. When he got to talking about her, she informed him that she was, in fact, that child of his. He looked at her longingly, his eyes filled with tears? *Oh, are you really that child of mine?* She pitied him in that poignant moment. But it was short-lived. Within moments, the curtain of senile dementia was again drawn over his eyes, and he forgot who she was, never to remember her again. The last time my sisters saw him, slightly before the turn of the century, he was yelling at Jatu, angrily asking her why she had let these strangers into his house. A few minutes later, he did not even remember that he had been yelling. Toumany died in September 2001. We were already in the US and did not go back for his funeral.

I was also six when I discovered video games. The biggest console on the block was the SNES. My favorite games were *Street Fighter II* and *Super Soccer*. I didn't own these games, but I had cousins who did. They were my Uncle Moussa's children. Uncle Moussa was the most successful of my father's siblings—he was the chairman and CEO of Petroci, the national oil company. At Christmas in the year that I was six, he gave me 25,000 francs, a sum I still remember. It might as well have been an inexhaustible supply of money to my young eyes. His generosity was legendary in the family. He had paid for one sibling to study in Europe, for another to study in the US. He had provided free housing for countless others. His name was uttered with awe and reverence. I worshiped my uncle from afar. It was the greatest compliment to me that people kept telling me that I looked like him, since I, too, had a protruding, ever-pouting lower lip. But with the benefit of adult perspective, there are questions I have to ask. How was my father chosen as the official dentist for Petroci? How did so many members of my extended family obtain positions within the company? I remember an incident in middle school where another boy accused my uncle of embezzlement. I was furious. I wanted to fight him. I am well aware of our long history of nepotism and of the personal fiefdoms that African leaders and their appointees carved out for themselves in the myriad administrative posts created after the end of colonization. These leaders amassed wealth, influence, and power for their families by ruling over vast systems of patronage. I cannot help but notice some uncomfortable similarities. I'm glad I didn't fight that boy.

But when I was six, all I knew was that my uncle was the greatest man in the family, that his children had the coolest toys, and that I wanted to play with them. And so, for much of my childhood, I spent weekends at my uncle's house. I played soccer, in which I was a passable goalie; basketball, at which I was utterly terrible; and all manner of video games. It was during these years that I fell in love with the German soccer team, since it was the best team in *Super Soccer*. And to this day, I root for Germany during the World Cup.

When I was six, I also acquired my lifelong fear of manhole covers. I don't walk on them. I'm afraid they'll fail to support my weight, and that I will rapidly fall to my death. I will walk around them or jump over them, but I will not, under any circumstances, step on them. This fear dates back to a visit to Kaniasso, my ancestral village. In Ivory Coast, no matter how long you've lived in a city, you're considered to have an ancestral village, which you're expected to visit now and then. Kaniasso was the seat of the Toron, the confederation of 13 villages my great-grandfather had once headed. I went there in 1992 with Uncle Moussa and his three sons. For us city kids, the place was a desolate hellhole with nothing to do. The unpaved roads were bumpy and dusty, and—horror of horrors—we had no video games. To make matters worse, the TV reception was terrible. My uncle decided to pay his respects to a village elder, and took us with him. My cousins took one look at the miserable shack of a dwelling and decided they would have none of it. They ignored my uncle's command to get out of the car. I was in a dilemma. I very much wanted to remain in the car with my cousins, but I was incapable of disobeying an adult, having been conditioned by years of corporal punishment. In the end, I took a look at my cousins, then another at my uncle, who was already walking away, and I stepped out of the car. *Now what?* Now I waited, impatiently watching my uncle and the elder have an interminable conversation in an inaccessible language.

It was while waiting that my mind began to wander and wonder. I mused that I was a soccer superstar. There I was, in the middle of a stadium, juggling a ball under the adulation and rapturous applause of the crowd. Hop, hop, hop. I went jumping backwards each time, hitting my imaginary ball, in perfect control, as if in defiance of gravity itself. Hop, hop, ho! I had stepped on a metal tile. But now I was losing my balance! Something was happening. Nothing good! It needed to stop. But it was too late. My entire world seemed to be crumbling. The ground was sinking. No, *I* was sinking, and fast. But how? And why?

I landed flat on my stomach. A piece of tile fell on me, nicking a small portion of my left ear in the process. I was still conscious. I opened my eyes and looked towards the sky. The ground seemed very far up. I prayed for help, but the only response was a profound silence. Seconds before, everyone had been so close. Now, it seemed like I was alone in the world at the bottom of my pit. I had fallen into a dry well, 12 meters deep. To the villagers, it had been clear that there was a well there. That's what the metal tile surrounded by three large rocks meant. But for me, a city kid, it had just meant was that there was a tile on the ground surrounded by a few rocks. Desperate over how I would ever get back out, I let out a loud wail. Immediately, my uncle's voice came thundering down. *Oh, you, shut up over there!* Another command from an adult. I obeyed.

I could see that on the walls of the well, some rocks stuck out farther than others. The walls could be scaled! Several people I didn't know and whom I would never see again came down into the well. They handed me up the human chain they formed until I was safely out of the well. It was then that I noticed that I was bleeding, mostly from my lower abdomen, where a strip of skin had been peeled off. All that remained was some white flesh, whiter even than the skin of those White people I had seen in movies. This pale patch was bleeding, and the blood would return anew each time it was wiped off. An ambulance was called and I was taken to the nearest city, Odienne. My memory is blurry after that. I remember the intravenous lines. I remember the extensive wounds in my lower abdomen. Were they ever going to heal? And if they did, would I have large, ugly scars that I would be forced to see every time I took a shower? I lost consciousness shortly after getting into the ambulance, and I have no idea how long I was hospitalized. I have no memory of being discharged and no memory of boarding a plane afterwards. But I do remember exiting the plane in Abidjan. My mother was waiting for me, and I've been told that she cried when she saw me, but I don't remember that either. In the end, my injuries had looked worse than they were. I hadn't broken a single bone and my wounds healed remarkably well in the following months. The only physical evidence that remains today is a small depression on the side of my left ear.

After the accident, my uncle took to calling me *le puisatier*, the French word for well digger. In a culture where children are not allowed to talk back to their elders, this became my nickname for many years, and I still occasionally hear that an uncle or aunt has inquired about the well digger. Although I am prone to laughing at myself in all sorts of situations, I can't quite reach the point where I can join in this joke. Falling into the well remains one of the scariest moments of my life. But the nickname is not the biggest scar I carry from this misadventure. People who have walked with me have noticed that I occasionally move to the side for no apparent reason. What they don't always know is that there is a method to the madness—I am actually avoiding manhole covers. They remind me too much of the metal tile that failed to carry my weight on that sunny day, so many moons ago, and I treat them with a respect and deference that will not allow me to step on them.

CHAPTER 6

Machiavellian

Herodotus wrote that Cyrus the Great, ruler of ancient Persia, told his subjects that "soft lands breed soft men." Whether or not the quote is accurate, it is reflective of a sentiment that has been common to many cultures throughout the ages. This is the idea that people forged in fire are more likely to withstand future adversity. This belief was very much a part of West African child-rearing when I was growing up. Corporal punishment was considered an integral part of a proper education. Parents, older siblings, and even teachers practiced it freely and liberally. There was only one man I knew who didn't beat his children. That man was Uncle Moussa, and because of this, it was often said, though never to his face, that his kids were spoiled.

In West Africa, Western parents who did not beat their children were often mocked for being too soft. The general belief was that children raised by White parents were ill-mannered and defiant of parental authority. This second point was particularly intolerable: children were to obey their parents in all circumstances. Even frowning was considered defiance. It is this particular attitude that makes me suspect that corporal punishment was not so much intended to toughen up kids, as parents claimed, but came from a Machiavellian belief that it is safer and more desirable to be feared than loved.

The earliest beating that I can recall must have been when I was about seven or eight years old. Like all the homes around it, our property was surrounded by a high wall. The entrance was through a large gate that opened onto a long driveway. On this particular day, I was playing with rocks on the driveway, throwing them around for my own amusement. My younger sister is seven years younger than me, and the sibling closest in age to me is six years older. Without playmates, I'd taken to inventing games on the fly for my own entertainment. So, there I was, enjoying my ability to send little rocks flying. But in my mirth and merriment, I'd neglected to tell those rocks that in no circumstances whatsoever were they to land on the windshield of the car parked on the other side of the gate at the end of the long driveway. It somehow came to pass that one of them did just that, seconds after I watched its parabolic arc trace its way above the gate, punctuating its landing with the celebratory sound of breaking glass.

My father was sleeping. I knew I was in trouble, but somehow hoped that I would escape a beating. Still, I prayed and hoped that he would sleep and sleep and just keep on sleeping. But my prayers were every bit as ineffectual as the amulets and incantations that African warriors had tried to use against European invaders. He woke up. I don't remember his anger. I don't remember what he told me. All I remember is that not long after he woke up, I was on my knees in his room, receiving blows from his belt on my back. There are some who say that corporal punishment is ineffective. This is probably true in the aggregate, but there are many children to whom it is a highly effective deterrent. I was one of them. I was terrified of being beaten. There would be no adolescent rebellion, in large part because if anyone threatened to tell my dad, I immediately turned into the meekest of sheep. But that was far into the future. Let's get back to the beating.

I could, as many children did, start wailing as soon as the first blow hit me. But I considered this deceitful and beneath me. Although I was afraid of being beaten, once someone started hitting me, I wouldn't cry. This would be interpreted by my parent as a sign that I hadn't yet been broken, and had therefore not learned my lesson. And so, my beatings were long. Or at least, that's how it felt. When my father let me go, I had indentations where the belt had landed so many times. And I had not cried! I smiled to myself. This would be worth bragging rights once I got to school.

Mothers, too, practiced corporal punishment. I was an upper-class child with a contempt for poorer people that is unfortunately very common in many children reared in privileg. We had a live-in maid and I recall wanting her to make me some fried plantains. It was 1 PM. Plantains were considered a snack, and snack time was 4 PM. But I wanted my plantains, and I wanted them now, even though the maid had told me she was busy. I was fond of knives and machetes. As a toddler, I'd had a huge temper that manifested in me running to the yard, grabbing a rusty machete—there was always one or two of those lying about—and running after my sisters, who would barricade themselves in their room.

I hadn't completely been cured of the habit by the time of the plantain demand, though it had become nothing more than a ritualistic way for me to express my anger and exasperation. On this day, there was no machete, so I grabbed a knife. I pointed it at the maid. She still wouldn't drop everything to make me some plantains, so I sliced her thumb. She promptly told my mom, and I was given a proper beating, though its memory has faded from my mind. I wouldn't beat a child, having spent more than half my life in the West, but I can't say that I didn't deserve to be beaten on that occasion.

My mother is also the person who administered the worst beating of my life, the one in which even I, with all my pride, could not help but be broken. I was around 11 years old and had asked my sister Sally to let me see her magazine and she had refused. My mom pleaded with her to let me see it, and she relented. I don't remember exactly what it was, but it was something like *Cosmopolitan* that is unlikely to be of interest to an 11-year-old boy. And so, I had no sooner taken a glance at it than I was through. I decided to toss it back onto the table, but it fell. In a condescending tone, my sister yelled, "Pick it up!" She was always gratuitously rude, and this time, I just didn't want to give her a victory.

"No!" I shouted back.

"Pick it up!"

"No!" I shouted again.

My mom, who had invested some social capital into getting my sister to let me see the magazine, now asked me to pick it up. I still refused. My pride was hurt. She threatened to grab her belt. I didn't budge. She brought the belt closer. I didn't budge. She hit me once, lightly. I didn't budge. She kept hitting me, again, and again, and again, each time asking me to pick it up. I still wouldn't. So, she switched to the buckle, and she hit me with it until it broke on me. Crying and just as broken as the buckle, I finally picked up the magazine and tossed it onto the table. Then I ran to my room, my tears still flowing.

Did these beatings constitute abuse? It would be unusual to find an African parent at that time who would have thought so. And because I was raised then and there, I never felt abused. These punishments were ubiquitous. Abuse for me would have meant punishment that was cruel and unusual. But, other than Uncle Moussa's children, I didn't know of anyone who wasn't beaten. In the ancient world, slavery was ubiquitous. There were people who thought that masters should not be needlessly abusive towards their slaves, but it did not seem to have occurred to anyone who cared to record it that slavery as an institution should be abolished. Not even Epictetus, who had himself been a slave, is known to have advocated universal manumission. And the same was true of beatings when I was growing up. Children might complain that a particular beating was excessive, but most of us never dreamed that there could be a world free of corporal punishment. This contributes to the difference in attitude between the modern West and much of the rest of the world on this topic. I would never call what my parents did abuse, though I am aware that other people see it that way. It did not result in me becoming prone to outbursts of anger and violence, and as far as I know, I have no psychological damage from it. I merely view it as a feature of my upbringing—unfortunate, but a common feature of its place and time.

The corporal punishment may not have left me with a scar, but there is one practice that has left a deep mark, although I wouldn't say that I suffer from it at this point. Again, I would not call this abuse either, but it is an illustration of the fact that African parents generally don't feel that they owe their children any sense of fairness. My sister Sally is six years older than I am, which entitled her to a bigger allowance when we were children. But she was a spendthrift, whereas I was a saver, and not infrequently she would borrow money from me after spending all of hers. She would come to me early in the morning, before school started, and plead with me to lend her a week's worth of my allowance on the promise that I would be repaid the same evening. The evening would come and there would be no mention of any money, as though I had dreamed up the entire thing. I would confront her about it, and she would give me some lame excuse and send me away.

I'd take my complaint to my mother, who would ask me to be kind enough to drop it, for the love that I bore her. I didn't have an expression for *no fucking way*, but I would emphatically refuse. I hadn't spent weeks saving just to give all of my money to someone with a bigger allowance than myself. This was unfair, very unfair. I would protest for all I was worth, and my mom would promise to pay me back if I let the whole thing drop. At this point, I'd be satisfied. I didn't care who paid me, so long as I got paid. Weeks would pass, then months, after which I would shyly bring it up to my mom.

At this point, instead of paying me back, my mom would tell me with a straight face that the money had gone towards my school uniform and supplies. I'd protest that this was not fair, that she hadn't told me that the money would be used this way, and that she would have bought my uniform and supplies anyway, irrespective of the promise she had made to pay me back. But she was both defendant and judge, and she would rule in her own favor, with no possibility of appeal. I would be sent away, with a keen sense that I had just been treated unfairly. I never brought it up to my father, because I expected him to find some way to blame me. And so, aggrieved though I was, I would keep my pain to myself and promise not to be so trusting next time. But I always had the sense that I was bad if I refused to help, and I confess to having fallen for this more than once as an adolescent.

And yet, much as I deplore this and other aspects of my upbringing, my mom sold all her possessions so that I could move to the US and become who I am today. Surely, I'm better off for having had her as a mother than not. But as an adult, though I am ready enough to give money, I never lend it to family members. It's just not worth the heartache.

CHAPTER 7

Mistress

There are some snapshots of moments in my childhood that I was too young to fully grasp at the time, but that now make me realize that things were far from rosy between my parents, even when I thought we were living in the best of times. The first such instance was when I realized that the word mistress didn't always mean what I thought it meant.

In French, the word *maîtresse* has two meanings. When my friends and I talked about our mistress, we were talking about our schoolteacher. But when I was about eight years old, I learned that my father also had a mistress. *This is very odd,* I thought. *He is so very grown, and he isn't going to any school that I know of. Why would he want a mistress, and what could she possibly be teaching him? And even stranger than that, why is my mother upset about it? Isn't learning supposed to be a good thing?* Things started to make a bit more sense when, over the following weeks, I started to understand that mistress can also refer to a woman who has a relationship with a married man.

I have another snapshot from around the same time. We lived in a villa with several bedrooms, one of which was the conjugal room, and one of which was my father's separate room—a man cave of sorts, where he kept his guns and his rifle. One day, very uncharacteristically, my mom was in this room. There was some screaming and a loud noise, but she had already left as I arrived. The phone was broken and on the floor. *Were they fighting?* My father picked up the phone and tried to put it back together. He showed it to me and chuckled, as if to say, "Look! She broke the phone! Women are really strange, my son, aren't they?" I nodded, as if to say "Yes, Dad. That is indeed very strange to attack a defenseless phone like that."

A third snapshot is from 1995 and 1996. My mom spent my childhood traveling the world, purchasing goods in bulk and selling them individually in Ivory Coast. At this time, she had traveled to the United States. This in itself was not so strange, but she was gone for three whole months. To 9-year-old me, that was a really long time! I heard from others that my father was not very happy about it. I missed her very much, but I assumed she must have had a perfectly rational reason for being away so long. Then she returned and surprised me by picking me up at school. I rushed to hug her. Some time later, I realized that she had moved out. She was living by herself in a small apartment in a different part of town. I got to spend time alone with her for a couple of days every other weekend. I loved those times. She cooked my favorite meals, including spaghetti with Toulouse sausage. She doted on me more than when she was living at home, but I wished she still lived with us. After a few months of this, she was back at home. My father told me that he had agreed to have her return home for the sake of us, the children. I didn't understand what exactly he meant, but I was glad she was back.

In retrospect, my parents' relationship appears very peculiar. It is not what I would want my marriage to look like. And yet, at the time, it didn't appear to be entirely out of the ordinary. Compared to their Western counterparts, women in Ivory Coast when I was growing up had very little power within their marriages. This wasn't just a matter of culture; it was rooted in economics, specifically in the disparity of economic opportunity between men and women. Boys were more likely to be schooled, and more likely to obtain a university education. This would result in a financial disparity between husbands and wives. Because husbands often earned so much more than their wives, it made sense for most women to be stay-at-home spouses. This, in turn, left them financially dependent on their husbands.

A woman in this situation would be trapped. Divorce laws were not friendly to women, who usually lost custody of any children and could expect no alimony. There was also very little opportunity to earn money, especially if the woman had been out of the workforce for years. Given these facts, most women opted to stay with an unfaithful spouse, or even a spouse who mistreated or beat them, rather than seek a divorce. But staying with such a spouse was not always an easy option. As a child, it was not uncommon for me to hear that such or such uncle had left his wife, or married his mistress, or taken a second wife—which Islam allows a man to do—even against the objections of his first wife.

So, in a way, my parents' marriage was somewhat typical for the time and place, and it was far from the worst of its kind. Thankfully, things are slowly changing in Ivory Coast. As more and more women are becoming more educated and financially independent, they are able to command more respect within their relationships. Still, as someone who believes in gender equality, I sometimes wonder what kind of romantic partner I would have become if I had never left.

CHAPTER 8

What Happened With Habib?

Our family was Muslim. In retrospect, it was a peculiar form of Islam that we practiced. My mom's Islam was devout but not scholarly. Though she prayed and fasted, she was a typical Ivorian Muslim in that she did not read nor understand Arabic. The wearing of the veil was strictly reserved for prayer time. My father was a rather liberal Muslim, perhaps because he had gone to Catholic school, perhaps because he studied in France, perhaps because of both. The result was a curious form of Islam where cured pork was a regular feature of our diet, and so was canned *cassoulet*, a French dish of pork and beans.

As long as we stuck to those and didn't eat "real pork"—whatever that meant—we felt that we weren't committing any infraction. And yet, this bothered me to some extent. When I was 10 or so, I resolved not to eat pork anymore. My father smiled and told me that I was free to do as I wished, but that this rule had originated at a time when people who ate pork incurred a higher health risk than we did in modern times, thanks to better sanitation. I was hungry. The food really was delicious. The argument proved very convincing, especially since I had secretly hoped to be convinced. I went back to eating cassoulet soon after.

More than once, my father told me that we were Muslims through a historical and geographical accident. The implication was that had we been born elsewhere or at a different time, we would probably be of another religious persuasion. And, like most religious people of their generation in Ivory Coast, my parents' faith was a syncretism that appended many indigenous African elements to their Abrahamic faith. This meant that we would celebrate Ramadan, but we would also make sacrifices to the spirits of the village, and we would wear amulets and perform ritual washings to ward off evil spirits. My father didn't seem to mind whether his children stayed Muslims. It seemed he cared more about keeping up appearances in front of our Muslim brethren. But what he did care about was that we believed in God. He was like a man who, having pushed a door ajar to his satisfaction, demands that it be pushed no further. But some doors, once opened, cannot ever be closed. He had been comfortable sending his children to Catholic school, as he himself had been schooled. But it led to unintended consequences in his children, most of whom pushed further on the door that he had unlocked and opened. For some, being confronted with a different religious tradition early in life reinforces their own beliefs. For others, it leads to a sort of religious relativism that can make them more open to conversion, or to drifting out of religion altogether. In my father's case, he emerged from Catholic school and his university days in France as a liberal, wine-drinking Muslim. As for his five children, only one of them is a practicing Muslim today, the others having found their way to Catholicism or out of religion entirely.

For many people, there comes a time when faith conflicts with rationality. Some people are able to somehow reconcile the two, but in my case, it slowly and inexorably led to irreligiosity. I've never discussed this with either of my parents, although my mother is aware of it because my sister Fatou revealed it to her in a moment of indiscretion. I had confided in Fatou because I had always seen her as a mini-mom, given that she is 12 years my elder. One day, Fatou and my mom were talking about faith. My mom had told Fatou about a video she had heard of, in which a Muslim man claimed that he could stump and silence any Christian with his probing questions. My mom shared that she wanted to test her own faith, and had inquired about whether there were similar videos that could stump Muslims.

Fatou was the first of my siblings to openly leave Islam. She had not just gone to Catholic school, she had gone to Catholic boarding school. There, she had seemingly found a new family and a deep sense of sympathy for Catholicism. Throughout my childhood, I could see a small poster of Jesus hanging on her closet door. So, it had not been much of a shock when she became a Catholic as an adult. My father was mostly worried about how our extended family would react. My siblings and I shrugged, thinking that she had already pretty much been a Catholic anyway. But my mom did not take it well at all. For her, it seemed like she had personally failed in her duty as a mother by not passing on her faith to her child.

Sometimes, I wonder if Fatou had let my secret slip because she subconsciously didn't want to be the only one judged for having left Islam. Regardless of her motives, when my mother mentioned that she was looking for a way to test her faith, she responded by saying that my mom should refrain from such tests, lest the same thing happen that had happened with Habib.

"What happened with Habib?"

Fatou tried to backpedal, but it was too late. The cat was already out of the bag. My mom was no idiot. She had seen me morph from a boy who would run to say his prayers several times a day into a young man who could never be bothered to pray or fast during Ramadan. My extended family was full of similar non-practicing Muslims, and so long as nothing was actually said about the matter, she had been able to assume that this was also what was going on with me. But now, it was clear that something had happened, and that Fatou knew what that something was.

By the end of their conversation, my mother knew that I had experienced a crisis of faith in my teenage years, after which I had briefly turned to Christianity before losing my religion altogether. Fatou called me afterwards to confess what she had done. She wanted me to call my mom and tell her that I had once questioned Islam but had returned to the fold and was now studying the Quran again. I felt deeply betrayed by my sister, but I had no time to dwell on that just yet. I was mortified and almost speechless. I can equivocate well enough to convince all kinds of people that I agree with them. But I am not a very good liar. This plan was never going to work. I didn't know how I could talk to my mom or what I could possibly tell her. She would never understand. She could never understand. Our culture made no room for direct disobedience to a parent. What if she decided to make a big fuss about it? What if she asked me to start praying again? I would be in the impossible situation of having to disobey a direct command, or having to make a promise I knew I would break. What if she no longer wanted to talk to me? It was one thing for her daughter to have left Islam for another Abrahamic religion. But I had rejected God entirely. This was the worst sort of apostasy, for which the prescribed punishment in Islam is death. Of course, my mom would not wish me dead, but pious as she was, would she still want to have a relationship with me? I was terrified. I stared at my phone again and again without being able to call. At last, after almost a week, my mom called me. We talked about her health. We talked about the weather. We talked about med school. We talked about my nieces and nephews. We did not talk about God, or religion, or prayer. I understood this to be a tacit agreement that we would never openly discuss my irreligiosity, and it was a deal I was happy to take.

Neither Fatou nor my mother ever told my father. African parents are not, by and large, interested in understanding their children's worldviews. Any such discussion inevitably devolves into lectures and admonitions. The wisest thing to do as a dependent child is to hide your thoughts, lest your parents punish you while telling themselves that they are doing it for your own good. And even after you acquire financial independence, it's best to let them assume whatever they wish to think about your beliefs. It's the path of least resistance, and the one I have chosen.

CHAPTER 9

An Ivorian Story

At first, the prosperity gave way to economic stagnation. Then, the high birth rates caused the stagnation to develop into a climate of interethnic strife, as more and more people fought over fewer and fewer resources. At last, the strife animated the passions of the masses and morphed into civil war. This could be the story of many poor, multiethnic nations around the world. But it's the story of Ivory Coast, the land I once called home. It is my story, the story of why my family and I decided to leave and settle in the United States.

Ivory Coast can broadly be divided into a forested southern half and a northern half dominated by savanna. The country is slightly bigger than New York State and is home to very different ethnolinguistic groups. It was conceived as an artificial administrative unit with boundaries that were created more because they were convenient to the French colonizers than because they made sense to the indigenous population. It became a state in 1960, without ever having been a nation. But because it was first established as a colony in 1893, it is all anyone currently alive has ever known, and it would be impossible to break it up or alter its borders without causing war and devastation on a massive scale.

The north–south divide in landscape also serves as a cultural and religious divide. The north is Muslim, and the dominant cultural group is called Mandinka or Mandingo. This is the same ethnic group that was the dominant force in the Mali Empire and the myriad petty kingdoms that succeeded it in the centuries after its collapse. In Ivory Coast, these people were historically primarily engaged in trade, so they are known by the Mandinka word for trader or merchant: *Jula*, sometimes spelled *Dyula* or *Dioula*. The current president of Ivory Coast, Alassane Ouattara, is the most prominent politician of this group, to which I also belong.

In the south, following a pattern established in many other West African nations, Christianity took root, likely because coastal territories were the most easily accessible to European colonizers and clergymen. The dominant cultural group in the south is the Akan group. They are related to the dominant group in Ghana, which borders Ivory Coast in the east. The dominant Akan subgroup in Ivory Coast is the Baoulé. The first president of Ivory Coast, Félix Houphouët-Boigny, was of this group. He reigned until his death in 1993, after which power passed to another Baoulé politician, Henri Konan Bédié, who had previously been the President of the National Assembly, the Ivorian legislature. There is a third group that needs to be introduced. The Bété come from south-central Ivory Coast. They have resided in the territory that later became Ivory Coast for longer, but have a smaller population than the other two groups. Laurent Gbagbo is the most prominent politician of this group.

Ivory Coast gained its independence in 1960, and was hailed as an economic miracle for more than 15 years afterwards. Even before then, it was by far the most prosperous colony in French West Africa. But with the replacement of White faces by Black ones at the top of the local political hierarchy, there came a new set of priorities. Dictators have long understood that one of the best ways to ensure a large base of support is to use corruption as a tool of governance. In such systems, there is an unspoken *quid pro quo*: The political class is permitted to embezzle almost at will and entrench itself in power at the local level, and in exchange, the ruler demands absolute loyalty. *Let us gorge ourselves and grow fat together*. Such is the unofficial political slogan.

Colonization had been a humiliating experience. There you were, in your own land, being ruled by foreigners who imperiously walked around as if they owned the place. You had to address them with honorifics while you endured the racial slurs they hurled your way. On top of that, they imposed a system of forced labor on you, and you were whipped if you refused to comply. And if one of those foreign overlords decided that they wanted to have their way with one of your sisters, there was little you could do. Starting in the late 1940s, many Africans began to agitate for independence. All manner of social ills came to be attributed to the hated colonial regime. If the country was poor, if our roads were unpaved, if there was no running water, if few could afford modern medicine, if literacy rates were low, and if the child mortality rate was high, it must be because of colonization. It must be because those Whites who ruled over us were plundering our wealth and sending it to their own country. What was needed was for us Africans to seize the destinies of our nations into our own hands, and all these ills would be cured.

But when independence came, few of our leaders seemed interested in working for the general welfare of the population. Instead, political office became primarily a means of enriching oneself. Each high office came with a vast system of patronage, where political allies and kinsmen could be nominated. With this, the allegiance of entire ethnic, tribal, and regional groups could be bought. It's possible to achieve a remarkably high degree of political stability with patronage politics. After all, what's the point of fighting when everyone can eat to their heart's content? But there are two problems with such systems. The first is that they require constant, massive economic growth to be sustainable. The second is that they tend to reward loyalty rather than competence, making it likely that sooner or later, economic mismanagement will take its toll. For as long as commodity prices remained high, Ivory Coast appeared to be well governed. Economic growth was fueled by a combination of agricultural exports and infrastructure spending. The government, hungry for qualified graduates, offered generous scholarships to any and every promising student. This is how my father was able to head to France and become a dentist.

But commodity prices came crashing earthwards from the stratospheric highs they had enjoyed in the late '70s, causing first an economic downturn, then a prolonged period of stagnation. This happened during a period of rapid population growth, which meant that all of a sudden, there was much less wealth to share among many more people. Industrialization had not been successful, and the vast majority of corporations were state-owned. In this context, the only secure path to wealth and prominence was through the control of government. Politics was devoid of any governing philosophy—it was simply a struggle for who would take the next turn at the trough. In such situations, ambitious politicians can often find an identitarian scapegoat, and this was the road Ivory Coast eventually took. While Boigny ruled, such divisions were kept under the lid. But after he died in 1993, his party immediately fractured along ethnic lines, much to the detriment of the country.

With this basic framework in mind, it's time to get better acquainted with some of the main characters in our drama. Ouattara obtained his PhD in economics at the University of Pennsylvania before working for the IMF, where he developed a reputation for integrity. Ivory Coast, like many other African nations that had run their economies into the ground, turned to the IMF for financing. As part of a Structural Adjustment Program, Ouattara became prime minister in 1990. This made him one of the most powerful men in the country. Northerners were thrilled to suddenly be so very near the pinnacle of power. But to many southerners in the ruling party, he was nothing but an interloper. He hadn't come up through the ranks. He hadn't shown any party loyalty. He hadn't even been chosen by Boigny. He'd been imposed from outside. And his program, which limited opportunities for kickbacks and imposed efficiency in government, was decidedly unpopular with those who had benefited from the existing system.

Boigny died in December 1993. I remember the day. I was seven years old, and the pomp and ceremony of the state funeral was the only thing shown on national television. It seemed to me that all the heads of states in the world were present for the occasion. Even when you turned off the TV, everyone was talking about politics. Specifically, they were talking about who would become president. I was raised in a northern household, and it was taken as a given that Ouattara should become president. He had been prime minister for almost three years. Unfortunately for him and for his supporters, the constitution was clear: the president of the National Assembly was the successor if the president died. This meant that Bédié should become president. Ouattara's appetite had been whetted, however, and he tried to make himself president. He lost the brief power struggle that ensued and was forced to resign. But there were only two years left on Bédié's term, with elections in 1995. Bédié knew that he wasn't particularly popular. And northerners were very excited at the prospect having one of their own as president. It was by no means a given that the election could be won if it was free and fair. But what to do?

What to do was to change the rules of the game to ensure that the election would not be free. If you're not sure whether you can beat your opponent, the easiest way to get rid of him is to have him disqualified on some pretense. Now, let's play African President! How can we disqualify an opponent with a reputation for integrity? What's that? We can put pressure on the National Assembly to pass a law to target him? Brilliant! Still, we must actually give some plausible justification. And what's this? His father is rumored to be from Burkina Faso? And he once accepted a scholarship reserved for students from Burkina Faso? Great! We can disseminate the idea that he is not Ivorian! He will be ineligible for the presidency because he is from Burkina Faso!

The law that was passed to target Ouattara stated that presidential candidates had to have parents who were both Ivorian, and they had to have resided in the country for five years preceding the election. Given that Ouattara had lived abroad, thanks to his years working as an IMF official, this law would have made him ineligible even if his citizenship were accepted. But the idea of disputing his nationality, born of electoral necessity, would prove to be one of the most divisive acts in Ivorian politics. Bédié could not know it at the time, but he was sowing the seeds of civil war.

Burkina Faso, formerly called Upper Volta, is a landlocked country to the northeast of Ivory Coast. Ouattara was born in Dimbokro, in central Ivory Coast, but his family has roots in both northern Ivory Coast and Burkina Faso. He spent a fair amount of his youth in Burkina Faso and does not speak French with an Ivorian accent. It was very easy for the charge that he was a foreigner to stick. The story of him receiving a scholarship reserved for Burkinabe students is a murky one. Reportedly, the quota of scholarship for Ivorian students had been filled, and his name was put forward thanks to the connections he had in Burkina Faso. An alternative version of this story is that his father was in fact a Burkinabe citizen, so it was no mystery that he qualified for the scholarship. Regardless of which of these stories is closest to the truth, in 1995, there was nothing he could do. The judiciary was not truly independent, so he had no recourse and was forced to watch the elections from the sidelines. The result was that Bédié was elected with 96% of the vote. He had had only one challenger—the leader of the very insignificant Ivorian Worker's Party. Another man who could have been a contender was Laurent Gbagbo, but he decided to sit out the election after judging it unfair. Few could imagine it at the time, but he too would become a major player in this tropical game of thrones.

Gbagbo was well known in the country for having contested the 1990 election, the first multiparty election held since independence 30 years earlier. This had been the price to pay for Western financial assistance, and Boigny had consented. Gbagbo, a talented politician from a small ethnic group, managed to get a respectable 18% of the vote. He had even managed to make a vocal supporter out of my sister Sally, who was then 10 years old. This was an amusing topic of conversation in our household when I was a kid.

Gbagbo had not entirely come out of nowhere. He was a historian by training, having obtained his doctorate from Paris Diderot University. And during the years of single-party rule, he had organized underground and built a following among university students. In 1982, he had gone into exile in France after organizing a teacher's strike. It wasn't until 1988, after political parties were legalized, that he was able to return. After losing the presidential election in 1990, he ran in the legislative elections and was elected to a seat in the National Assembly. Did he boycott the 1995 elections out of solidarity with Ouattara? Or was it because he feared he would suffer another defeat? No one knows. But it is notable that at this stage in his career, he was unwilling to participate in an election that was not free and fair.

⁂

In the years after independence, Ivory Coast became known as a land of immigration. It attracted large numbers of immigrants, many of them from Burkina Faso, during its years of prosperity. Culturally, these newcomers tended to associate with the Jula. And so, over time, in the minds of southerners, links were established between Ouattara and foreigners, and between foreigners and Jula. It did not help that the country had no *jus soli*—that is, no birthright citizenship. This meant that people whose grandparents had moved to Ivory Coast were still considered foreigners. In the 1998 census, 26% of the population was counted as foreign. As the year 2000 approached, it became clear that Ouattara would again not be allowed to run. As an added precaution against the northern vote, the Jula started being denied national ID cards, which were required to vote. We had now become second-class citizens. My sister Sally, who was 18 years old in 1998, had to jump through numerous hoops and fight for several months to be granted an ID card.

Political instability is a regular feature of many countries in this region, but it had somehow spared Ivory

Coast until the turn of the century. Troops in Abidjan had been agitating for better pay and living conditions. In December 1999, as their demands were ignored, the agitation became a mutiny, and the mutiny morphed into a coup. Before we could understand what was happening, the president had been toppled. Many of us were ecstatic. When foreigners told us that coups usually led to dictatorships and political strife, we were dismissive. That may have been true elsewhere in the world, we thought, but Ivorians were by nature a peace-loving people. We didn't consider that Ivory Coast had only existed for a century, and that there was no such thing as an Ivorian nature. Instead, the fact that the coup had occurred without any bloodshed seemed to support our assertion. Surely, we thought, there could never be instability here.

At first, the military junta promised free and fair elections. Its leader, Robert Guei, was a retired general who was generally well liked. He repeated to anyone who would listen that he was not a man ambitious for power. He was going to organize elections and fade from the scene. He had only come to sweep the house. But, having swept the house, the Sweeper—as he came to be known—found that it was rather to his liking. What was the point of spending all this time and energy sweeping a palace clean so that someone else could enjoy its use? A new constitution was drafted, and Guei decided to eliminate his main competitors. A provision was included stating that candidates had to have four Ivorian grandparents and never to have taken another nationality. These provisions targeting Ouattara were submitted to a referendum. Ouattara was in a bind. If he called for his supporters to vote no, he would be tacitly admitting that he did not meet the qualifications. Besides, there was the added risk of losing, which would be devastating for his prospects. So, he declared himself targeted but unconcerned, and called for a *yes* vote. The referendum was adopted.

But before Outtara could run, he had to be declared eligible by the Constitutional Council. One by one, on national TV, 14 would-be candidates were eliminated, including Ouattara for not being Ivorian enough and Bédié for immorality. In the end, Gbagbo was the only leading politician allowed to run. Guei thought he could beat him, but it would prove to be a mistake. Gbagbo won the October 2000 election with more than 60% of the vote, taking the support of those who would have preferred to vote for the eliminated candidates. Guei tried to claim that he had, in fact, won the elections, but the population took to the streets. The armed forces were ordered to fire on demonstrators, but most of them sided with the civilians and Guei was forced to step down. The very next day, Ouattara's supporters took to the streets again to demand new elections. They were met by Gbagbo's supporters, who had the support of the armed forces that had sided with them the day before. In the clashes that ensued, civilians were killed: 57 bodies were later found in a mass grave on the grounds of a mosque in Abidjan's Yopougon district. It became known as the charnel house of Yopougon. It was an inauspicious start to a presidency.

Laurent Gbagbo knew how shallow his support was. Most of the country had seen the election as a farce—only 37% of registered voters had bothered to participate, and among those 11% had returned blank ballots. Gbagbo even stated that he had become president amid calamitous circumstances. Yet there he was, baffling all the naysayers who had called him an eternal opponent. He had been treated as something of a joke, and now the joke was on his detractors. Nevertheless, his supporters were emboldened. Youth militia groups formed to intimidate the opposition through acts of violent repression. During my last school year in Ivory Coast, 2000 to 2001, I suddenly became very conscious that I was a northerner. It didn't matter that I didn't speak Jula and had been born and raised in the south. Tribalism had never made sense to me. I had known that my family had northern origins, but this had never meant much to me, except that I was a Muslim, and therefore didn't take communion at Mass in my Catholic school. But now, as the new regime tried to secure its hold on power, a climate of xenophobia descended on the nation. In the streets, on the evening news, and even at school, there was open talk of teaching those pesky foreigners and northerners—who were often considered one and the same—a lesson they wouldn't forget. People also spoke of a day of reckoning, and of how true patriots would not shy from lending their hands to the task of taking their country back. Hearing people I had played soccer with engage in such talk, and imply that they, too, would enthusiastically participate in whatever that day of reckoning might entail, was unnerving, to say the least. I became adept at avoiding the subject of politics. What if a day of wrath and reckoning did come and I was remembered as a vocal northerner? Would some of my classmates decide that I, too, was one of those pesky foreigners who needed to be taught a violent lesson? It was safest to keep silent.

But in my heart, along with my fellow northerners, I found the new president illegitimate. Part of it was the fact that Ouattara hadn't been allowed to run. But the other part was this business of the charnel house. Investigations into the deaths seemed to be going nowhere. And when a trial finally did take place, witnesses were intimidated. To this day, many supporters of Gbagbo feel that the accounts of these deaths were made up. These events sowed the seeds of division. Within two years, the simmering tensions had given way to a civil war, born out of a rebellion that started in the north of the country. By this time, my family had already left for what we hoped would be greener pastures.

This background of economic mismanagement and gradual descent into civil war was the main factor that pushed us out of Ivory Coast. Seeing the writing on the wall, people who could afford to leave did so. My mom gathered her resources and sold all she had to purchase plane tickets for her children and herself. There was only so much money she could raise. And so, she had to make the agonizing choice of bringing only her two youngest kids: my little sister, a month shy of eight, and 15-year-old me. When my father tells the story of why he moved to the US, he depicts it as a hard decision he made for the sake of his children. He abandoned his dental office, gave up his life as a prosperous dentist, and moved to the US in order to shepherd his children to a more successful life than they could have had otherwise. Doubtless, he does not intend to deceive anyone, but this picture is not quite complete. I was young, but not so young that I don't remember that the decision to move was my mom's, and that my father was initially strongly opposed. In fact, he was so opposed that he didn't contribute financially to the move. So opposed that he didn't move with us, but several weeks later. So opposed, in fact, that after joining us he went back after about a month. So opposed that I can vividly remember an exchange between us in our early days in the US.

I am alone with my father. He is reproaching me for not protesting when my mom made the decision not to return to Ivory Coast. I take refuge behind my age, telling him that I am only 15, and that the decision isn't mine. My father is not convinced. He tells me that I am old enough to be able to tell right from wrong, and that I could have told my mom that we should go back. I repress the laughter that is building within me. *Dude*, I want to say, *do you really expect me to turn down a chance to live in the United States?* But I say nothing. We might be in the US, but directly challenging a parent is still not allowed in my culture.

Looking back, I'm puzzled by why my father left to go back to Ivory Coast. This was before the war had started, so he may have been hoping that things would get better. As for why he came back, I can see now that the family fortunes had taken a turn for the worse in the preceding decade. First, we had moved from a large villa in a nice neighborhood to a small apartment in a rundown neighborhood. Likewise, my father's dental office had moved to a less impressive building in the administrative district of Abidjan. There was no longer a chauffeur, as there had been when I was very young. And the cook who had once lived with us left at some point, never to be replaced. All we had left was only one maid. We were still members of the middle class, and perhaps even on the lower rungs of the upper class, whatever that meant, but clearly these were lean years. When people are hungry, dental care becomes a luxury fewer and fewer can afford. We could also no longer count on Uncle Moussa's legendary generosity. Bédié's ascent to the presidency had meant a loss of power for northerners, many of whom found themselves replaced by regime loyalists. My uncle's positions of Chairman and CEO of Petroci, the national oil company, came with significant patronage opportunities, and were therefore very sought after. At some point in the mid '90s, my uncle was ushered out, and he could no longer play the role of universal benefactor for our very large extended family.

A lot of people assume that when a person seeks refuge from political instability, they will simply find the closest border and seek admission into the country on the other side. But the conditions of would-be asylees are varied. Some leave at the dawn of instability, while others leave at the last possible minute. The earlier that a person leaves, the more room there is for economic considerations. In those cases, it isn't merely a case of moving away from war. Rather, it becomes a matter of moving where your family is most likely to thrive. So what factors pulled us towards the United States?

It's hard to overstate how large the US looms in the imagination of many people all over the globe. As a child, when I thought of America, it wasn't just a country—it was an idea and a dream. It was the land of universal freedom. It was the land of the triumph of the civil rights movement. It was the land of economic opportunity. It was the land of justice, even for the little guy. It was the land of meritocracy. It was where all the best movies were made. It was where all the famous singers were from. It was the ultimate force for good in the world. I thought that moving to America was everyone's dream and that to live there was to win the life lottery. But the idea that I, a complete nobody from a third-world country, might be granted the chance to move there seemed so far-fetched that I would not even allow myself to hope for it.

There is one way in which I am unequivocally my father's son—I am very risk averse. I don't take chances when the odds of success are low. I am more acutely in touch with my fears than I am with my hopes. If I think a door is locked, I will not try to open it. When starting on a venture, all I can see are the pitfalls and the thousand ways in which failure is likely. Aware of my strengths, I am careful to only pick fights I am reasonably certain to win. Moving to America is not something I would have done. But thankfully, it was my mother who was the decision maker. She is a woman who takes counsel of her hopes rather than her fears. She will push on doors that appear locked. When she imagined moving to America, she would talk of owning a taxicab in New York, and how much money she could make. She did not know anything about what it took or how much it cost to own a cab. She didn't know how expensive the medallions were. She didn't know about the operating expenses. But the idea that things would go well helped her decide to make the move rather than succumb to the paralysis by analysis that would have gripped my father or me.

We left Ivory Coast on July 31, 2001. We spent the night in Accra, Ghana, then flew into New York the next day. Our destination was Southfield, Michigan, a suburb of Detroit. My mom knew a Liberian woman named Dimanche who lived there. The plan was that we would stay with her until we could afford to be on our own. We imagined this would be no more than a couple of months, but we ended up staying there for our first six months in the US. Of course, there would be no yellow cab in Michigan. The dreams of an easy life faded rather quickly, in fact. And slowly, it dawned on us that for all the potential benefits of life in America, we were now squarely at the bottom of the socioeconomic ladder. If we had known lean times in the preceding decade, the years ahead promised to be leaner still.

CHAPTER 10

A Barbarian în Rome

My first visit to the US was in 1999. It was a summer trip
that had been financed by Uncle Moussa, our ubiquitous
benefactor. My father had asked him to take me with his
family as a reward for my good grades. I had done rather
well that year, getting at some point a perfect score in
German for the entire trimester. Since getting good
grades was my primary responsibility, it was decided
that I should receive some kind of recompense, as an
encouragement and an incentive for further academic
accomplishments. It was a deal I was glad to take, unsure
as I was of my abilities in any other domain. As an earlier
reward my father had given me a computer, which had
been my most ardent desire, and which quickly became
my best friend. And now, there was this, a trip to the
USA—the country everyone dreamed about but few were
lucky enough to actually visit. I couldn't be more elated to
be among those select few.

Sometimes, I wonder what nomadic barbarians
such as the Huns felt as they entered Rome and beheld
its monuments. Were they impressed by the grandeur?
Were they apprehensive as they marched through such
unfamiliar surroundings? Or were they simply confused
by some of the technology an average Roman would

have taken for granted? This last issue was the first puzzle I encountered, in the restrooms of JFK airport. I could not for the life of me figure out how to operate those damn faucets. I stared at them for a few minutes, but to no avail. *Where in the world was the handle?* After scratching my head for an eternity—metaphorically, that is, since I wouldn't have dreamed of doing so with my hands still unwashed—I happened to place my hands where the infrared sensor could detect them, and to my surprise the water started flowing. I washed my hands with my mouth agape. It was my "Welcome to America" moment.

We didn't linger long in New York, soon heading to Madison, Wisconsin, where Uncle Soumaila—the Jula version of the Arabic name Ismail—lived with his wife and baby daughter. He was my paternal grandmother's youngest son, and it seemed to us teenagers that he mostly did four things: work night shifts, sleep during the day, smoke, and drink Pepsi. He never seemed to be in a great mood when he was awake, so we mostly tried to stay out of his way. This wasn't too hard, since Uncle Moussa had rented an apartment for us. There were two great things about that apartment. First, we did not have any adult supervision, which meant that we could go to bed whenever we wanted, cook—or rather, attempt to cook—whatever and whenever we wanted, and play without interruption. Second, the apartment had a game room with a PlayStation. If you had asked me to design a perfect vacation, I couldn't have done better.

But it wasn't all fun and games. Uncle Moussa didn't want us to spend the summer doing nothing and forget everything we had learned in school. He wanted us to keep learning—specifically, he wanted us to use the opportunity of being in the US to practice our English, so he hired a tutor. Her name was Jennifer Eck, a tall brunette woman whom we immediately had hopeless fantasies about. She was 27 years old, had studied French in college, and had a boyfriend who played the guitar or some other instrument. I don't remember much about the boyfriend, and I never met him. I just remember thinking what a lucky bastard he was.

We had two types of sessions with Jennifer. Sometimes we practiced at the apartment. She would give us short lessons, after which we answered questions in a grammar book. Since French grammar is much more complicated than English grammar, this wasn't too difficult. The other thing we did with Jennifer was go into town and practice speaking English. I think this was by far the most useful thing she did for us. She even took us bowling, which was a ton of fun and an experience unlike anything I'd ever experienced in Ivory Coast.

Jennifer taught me that my last name, pronounced *fa-NEE* like *the knee*, shared its spelling with a word that meant butt. *But, but, that can't be*, I thought. I thought wrong, it seems. It was probably the worst news I got on my entire trip. I felt like a laughingstock, the butt of all jokes, so to speak. If there were any reason I was thankful to return to my country after the summer, it was because no one in Ivory Coast would look at my name and imagine that it meant anything like rump. Today, though, I am thankful that I moved to the US rather than the UK, given what *fanny* means over there. But at age 13, I didn't know this other meaning, and it would have been scant consolation.

The rest of the summer went rather well and I learned to appreciate Madison, with its organized mass transit system. Ivorian buses were always crowded and only used by the poor. I learned to love the fries and milkshakes at Culver's. I learned what a Happy Meal was when I pretended to understand the girl at the counter and said yes to whatever she was asking me. I realized to my horror that she had been asking whether I wanted the toy that went with the meal when she gave it to me. I walked away ashamed and wondering what she thought of my intelligence.

One last experience is worth recounting. I walked outside our apartment one day in September, only to find that in the shade, it was much cooler than I had expected. In fact, this was the coldest thing I had ever experienced, the only comparable thing being air-conditioned rooms in which the temperature had been set low. I was within a couple of yards of the apartment door, and so I concluded that this must be due to the air conditioning inside. Everything in America was so much more powerful than I'd ever encountered. I mean, even the air conditioning was so strong that you could feel it outside the building! I was already thinking of how I would explain this to people back home and wondering whether they would believe me. But, as I kept walking, and getting further and further away from the door, I realized that this was the actual weather. I didn't want to believe that it could be this cold, but I had to concede that there was no other explanation. In retrospect, it must have been in the high

60s Fahrenheit in the shade, a fact that makes me smile when I recall this event. But at the time, although I had seen snow on TV, I could not imagine how it could possibly be colder than what I was feeling. I didn't know that two years later I would move to the US, and that winter was coming.

CHAPTER 11

Mockingbird

Dimanche was in her 40s, I think. She had three children, the oldest of whom was Greg. Like me, he was born in 1986. He became my first American friend. Greg had a form of developmental delay that was mild enough for him to be able to graduate from high school, but pronounced enough that most of his friends were children much younger than him. In between playing video games and discussing school, I peppered him with questions about the English language, much to his annoyance. Learning English was my preoccupation in those early days. At my school in Ivory Coast, I had been one of the best students in English class. But here in America, I found to my dismay that being able to write short paragraphs was useless when it came to having conversations. True, I had memorized the past tense and participle of many irregular verbs. True, I could tell you about cats, big black cats, and big black cats over and under a table, but this was rarely relevant when I was trying to order food or talk to people at school.

I could see that people who had been in the US for a long time, regardless of their age or education, were much more fluent than me. Speaking English was so hard that it seemed fluency was something accessible to every immigrant but me. Every conversation was torture. I had to think in French, translate the individual words into English, and rearrange them, before finally voicing them. It was very tedious. For a boy who was as talkative as I had been, it seemed that some spell of mutism had been cast on me. *Will things ever go back to normal? Will I ever be able to converse again?* My preferred remedy, then as now, was to intellectualize my problems. Thankfully, this was a problem that lent itself well to intellectualization. I decided that I would get my hands on as many books as I possibly could.

My new school was Southfield-Lathrup High School, which no longer exists. When I attended, it was a pretty diverse school with large numbers of Whites, Blacks, and immigrants from all over the globe, but especially from Africa and Iraq. Because of this, there was a pretty strong English as a Second Language Program. Foreign students would be tested, then placed into one of four ESL levels. When you reached ESL IV, you could concurrently take English classes with the kids who had English as a first language. I placed into ESL IV. This meant that I was in regular English but took my social studies classes with ESL kids. In social studies, we learned about the topics American kids normally covered in middle school. There was also a huge emphasis on English grammar. Although I was technically a junior, the regular English class that I was placed in was a 10th-grade class. During my first month, I had to read both *Julius Caesar* and *To Kill a Mockingbird*.

Shakespeare was more accessible to me than Harper Lee's novel. This was perhaps not so surprising, as I would learn that there had been a large influx of French words into the English language after the Norman Conquest in 1066. The further back in time I looked, the more written English had words that seemed to be plucked directly from my native language. So, the Latinate words that swarmed over the pages of Shakespeare were much more accessible to me than the Anglo-Saxon words in normal speech. I was sent to the dictionary again and again to look up such words as "porch" or "thus." It was a slow undertaking. To this day, I have no idea what *To Kill a Mockingbird* is about. My reading of it was much too interrupted for me to derive any kind of greater meaning from it. I can only remember a few things from this classic of American literature. There was a man named Atticus, who was a lawyer and presumably did lawyery things. And there was a Black guy who presumably had a name, and who was accused of some stuff, probably of a criminal nature. People in the American South said "yonder." There was no bird, but if there was a bird, he didn't do any mocking that I can remember. It didn't register in my mind that Atticus was named Finch, or that a finch was a kind of bird. There was also the little girl who was the narrator. Her name was Scout, I believe, though that must have been a nickname. There was a trial at some point. I believe Atticus, the lawyer, was defending the Black guy with the name, but I don't remember whether he was acquitted, though I assume he was. I have been told that it really is a great book, and that I should give it another try, now that my command of English has improved. But, truth be told, I'm afraid I have some kind of PTSD about that book. The experience of plowing through it was so traumatic that I would have given up on the English language if it had been an option.

But I was now living in an English-speaking country and there was nothing to do but keep going.

Slowly, things got better. *I* got better. I decided to start with easier, shorter books. There were usually two dictionaries at my side, one of which was a French–English translator. I remember reading books like *Hatchet* and *The Prophet*. The more I read, the more words I acquired. And the more words I picked up, the more I could focus on the plot and meaning of the story, instead of having my head sent back and forth like a ping-pong ball between the book and the dictionary. I also subscribed to an email list that sent me one vocabulary word a day. The progress was slow, but it was definitely noticeable after a year, at least at the written level. But for all my increasing ease with a pen, my conversational skills were still sorely lacking, and I found myself retreating from conversations. The following scene occurred many times in my first year.

"Hey, man, what d'ya think of the game last night?"

"Excuse me, cood you pleez repeet wat you sayd?"

"I said what d'ya think of the game last night?"

"Uh, soree, uh, a leetle beet slower, pleez?"

"The game. What d'ya think? You watched the game, right?"

"Oh, yeah. Hahaha."

Then I would quickly walk away, hoping that my response had not been too inappropriate. It was evident that my English wasn't good enough to understand what was being said to me, and I didn't want to have my poor interlocutor repeat what they had said a fourth time. Fortunately for me, over time, these instances became less frequent.

CHAPTER 12

Hamed

For about a semester in high school, I lived with my cousin Hamed in Maryland. I was 16 years old, and Hamed was 35. At the time, he had lived in the US for about half his life. He had been a stellar student as a youth, but had then become estranged from his mother as a young adult, and she had subsequently stopped supporting him financially. So, in spite of the promise he had once shown, his life had become one of hardship. Bearded and prematurely balding, he was also tall, slim, gregarious, charismatic, and exceedingly opinionated. He was one of those people who could make you feel that they had unlocked the key to success in America. A conversation with my mom and me was all it had taken. We were sold on the idea of me living with him. He had been in the country for longer and could likely help me navigate high school and college applications.

At the same time, my mom was trying to move to Florida, far from the Michigan cold. Moving somewhere new with two kids seemed risky. But with one less mouth to feed, she might just be able to pull it off. And so, it was decided. My mom took my little sister to Florida, to pursue some projects I was never informed about, and I went to live with Hamed, whom I had last seen when I was three years old. Somehow, he recognized me when he picked me up at the airport. He was affable and talkative as he took to me his two-bedroom apartment in Laurel, Maryland. I was a devout Muslim at the time and I had brought my prayer rug with me. Hamed was the only conspicuous Christian in my entire extended family. He was not happy to see that rug in his house. My first night there, he told me that he was going to tell me all about Islam. I was skeptical. What was there to tell me? If he thought he could sway me away from the right path with his pretty words, he was going to be sorely mistaken.

My adherence to Islam was founded in logic, not in faith, though I did not realize it at the time. It was logical to me that there was only one God, logical to me that he had created humankind, and logical to me that he should speak to his creation through prophets. It was also logical that at some point, he had reached the end of what he wanted to communicate and transmitted his final message to Muhammad, seal of the prophets. What did not seem logical was that God could have a son, or that he should need to send this son as a sacrifice, presumably to himself, if he decided that a sacrifice were needed for him to forgive humanity its innumerable sins.

The first independent thought I recall having about God and religion happened when, at 10 years old, I came up with a version of Pascal's Wager. I took it for granted that a deity would demand my faith. And it made sense to me that it was a lesser calamity to believe in a non-existent God, and to have therefore wasted only prayer time, than to fail to believe in an existent God and condemn oneself to eternal torment. Around this same time, I also realized that, unlike my siblings and everyone else I had ever met, I didn't find atheism utterly incomprehensible. In fact, although I disagreed with its premise, I recognized that it was a position extremely easy to defend on strictly logical grounds.

So, it was with this worldview that I encountered Hamed a few days after I had moved in with him. He was armed with articles critical of Islam that he had found online. In retrospect, they were taken from an Islamophobic evangelical Christian website. The literature advanced the notion that Arabs had been polytheistic before the advent of Muhammad. They outlined the idea that Allah had been a deity in a pantheon of gods. They said that because the father of Muhammad was named Abdallah, which means the slave or servant of Allah, polytheistic Arabs were already worshiping Allah. What Muhammad had done, then, was merely declare that all other gods but this one were false. Much later, I would learn that, although no one disputed the polytheism of the ancient Arabs, this conception of Allah as a god within their pantheon was not universally accepted. But at the time, it was enough to shake my convictions to the core. It seemed to me that this cheapened God. It was as though someone had looked at the Greek pantheon and decided that Zeus was the only true God. This couldn't be. Islam, I decided, could not possibly be right.

There had been two main religions in Ivory Coast: Islam and Christianity. And without realizing it, as a Muslim kid educated in Catholic school, in a country that was split almost equally between Muslims and Christians, I had absorbed along with my religious assumptions a dualistic worldview in which one or the other religion must necessarily be true. And so, when I decided that Islam was wrong, it was self-evident to me that Christianity must be right. This is how, in the 16th year of my life, having put aside the religion of the crescent, I came to take up the religion of the cross and accept Jesus as my personal Lord and savior. This would almost certainly never have happened if I had not left the country of my birth. I had moved to a new country, and like a transplanted tree absorbing features of its new soil and environment, I was slowly acquiring a new identity and transforming into something new. And it wasn't only true in the realm of religion.

CHAPTER 13

African în America

What does it mean to be Black? Does it mean anything at all? Is Blackness a matter of complexion, or is it a matter of culture? And if it's a matter of culture, which culture exactly? Is there such a thing as Black culture? And if there is, is there such a thing as White culture? For many people who have grown up in the US, the answer is that to be Black is to be African American, to be a descendant of the slaves forcibly torn from their continent and shipped across the ocean to a country that would oppress them and suppress their every aspiration. To be Black is to be the intellectual heir of such luminaries as Frederick Douglass, W.E.B. Du Bois, and James Baldwin. It is an experience and identity inextricably linked to the history of chattel slavery, America's original sin. To be Black is to see life through the prism of a never-ending struggle for racial justice that began with the long fight for abolition and persists today under the guise of criminal justice reform.

But growing up in West Africa, I had a much different notion of my Blackness, which was first and foremost something that rarely came up. Whereas in the crucible of America's racial caste system, Blacks underwent an alchemy in which the various identities and cultures of their ancestors were melted and melded into one, for Africans the concepts of Blackness and Africanity are European imports. Before colonization, people primarily saw themselves as Fula or Yoruba or Wolof or Bamileke, and would be both bemused and amused to hear that they were one people. Sure, they could see that their skin was dark, especially in comparison to Europeans and Arabs, but wasn't almost everyone of dark complexion? The idea that there was something called Africa, and that they were therefore Africans, was not part of their worldview. People in different parts of Africa felt no more of a sense of kinship towards one another than the Portuguese feel towards Latvians.

But colonization intervened, and, under the yoke of foreign domination, many of those dark-skinned peoples in sub-Saharan Africa began to develop a sense of brotherhood born of their common purpose of achieving independence. But independence was no sooner achieved than tribalism reasserted itself stronger than ever. Almost all of the new nations born in the 20th century found within themselves ethnic groups with little affinity for one another, all competing for political power and the wealth it brought. It was in such an environment that I was born, and Blackness, whether mine or that of anyone else around me, was an afterthought that only came up when people of European descent happened to be in the picture, which was seldom. All the people I liked, all the people I disliked, all my teachers, all the engineers, all the physicians, all the lawyers, and all the government officials were Black. Blackness did not and could not act as a differentiator of anything.

If Blackness meant anything to me, it was the broadly shared worldview I observed among all those ethnic groups all over the continent. This was a pronounced social conservatism that embraced faith in the divine, corporal punishment, and the sort of moralism that preaches personal responsibility as the panacea for all social ills. In this worldview, the solution to larceny was that thieves simply needed to stop stealing, and the solution to murder was that murderers should stop murdering, and in each case, punishments should be as harsh as possible in order to dissuade these malefactors. In this worldview, homosexuality was a great sin, detrimental to the moral fiber of society. It was equally evident that the solution to the perceived problem of homosexuality was to victimize gay people until they learned the error of their ways. And if teenagers were having sex, it was probably because their parents had done a poor job of instilling religious morals, and the solution was to shame them and bring them towards God. These attitudes were so pervasive that they were shared by men and women, by Muslims and Christians, and by old and young alike.

There are two images of Black America that are prevalent in Africa. The first is that of the civil rights struggle. Martin Luther King Jr. is universally known and revered, and so is the name—though not necessarily the face—of Rosa Parks. These images have enormous resonance because Africans whose parents lived through the fight for independence can easily see in them brothers and sisters united by blood and by a common struggle for justice and equality. But there is a second image of Black America that evokes very different feelings. This is the depiction of gangsters, which is ubiquitous in movies and music videos. Here, the African is torn. On one hand, everyone can recognize the cool factor of those larger-than-life figures surrounded by guns, money, and attractive, scantily clad women. On the other hand, there is a lot in this image for a socially conservative African to deplore. The result is a sense of ambivalence about Black Americans, similar to the ambivalence one might feel about a brother who has moved far away and who has changed so much that it's hard to relate to him. You still consider him your brother, but certain aspects of his life make you frown.

What happens, then, when you go visit this long-lost brother of yours and realize that he is in many ways struggling? What do you conclude is the cause of his difficulties? If you are a moralist, you will immediately blame the things you dislike in your brother, and this is precisely the reaction the new African immigrant usually has towards Black Americans. He asks who are these so-called African Americans who know so little of Africa, and who have retained nothing of African culture. He asks why so many of them are unemployed when he who has just arrived has found a job. He asks why so many of them are in jail for drug-related offenses. He wags his finger and formulates a diagnosis that is harsh and unsparing. African American culture is ill, its children having both unmoored themselves from the moral values of African culture, and failed to anchor themselves to the best of Western culture. The African American remains poor in a land of opportunity because he is lazy and addicted to blaming others for his own failures. The African American lags in academic achievement because he is more interested in sports and entertainment than in scholarship.

The African prescription for this malady is:

Pull your pants up, put the ball down, pick up a book, study, and stop whining. Jim Crow was a long time ago, and slavery even more so. No one ever whipped you, no one ever made you pick cotton, no one ever sold your children, and no one ever told you to go to the back of the bus. The opportunities that you have in the US are greater than those you would have if you had been born Black almost anywhere else. So, stop complaining and go get a job. It is because of your behavior that some people are racist. You are giving us all a bad name.

This is the voice of the newly arrived African—the long-lost brother is no sooner found that he is repudiated. It is no surprise that many African immigrants find their home in the Republican Party. And it is also no surprise that, given my sense of alienation from Black American culture, I should have felt very strongly that I was an African in America rather than an African American.

CHAPTER 14

A Black Guy Who Just Happens to Have Done Some Stuff

What does it mean to be Black in a country with lots of Black people who are not Black like you're Black? How do you find your identity as a 16-year-old expatriate? Who do you relate to and what role models do you find? All I felt towards contemporary African American culture was a deep sense of alienation. I was not one of them. I would never be one of them. And they seemed to think that, because my conversational skills in English left a lot to be desired and because I was from Africa, I must be an idiot. The contempt was mutual. But, as a rule, it was much easier for me to relate to African Americans of earlier generations than to the people I was going to school with. Where was the culture of Richard Wright and James Baldwin? Why was there so little of Maya Angelou yet so much of R. Kelly? Why was there no longer anyone like Ralph Ellison and Zora Neale Hurston? Where had the Black public intellectuals gone, and who had risen to take their places? I could not see them. And because I could not see them, I assumed they didn't exist.

Many African Americans see African immigrants as both arrogant and hopelessly deluded about the state of racial relations in the US. They don't take kindly to foreigners who have the audacity to lecture them about personal responsibility when they understand nothing about the reality of growing up as a minority in a country where opportunity has historically not been equitably distributed. They emphatically point out that the reason their culture isn't African is because their ancestors did not travel to America on a cruise ship, but that they were violently ripped from their continent and way of life and sent to a faraway land where they had to survive as best they could. They feel pride in the many exports of African American culture over the decades and reject the notion that theirs is a culture that is somehow inferior to any in Africa.

The African immigrant who seeks to distance himself from them appears like an Uncle Tom—so preoccupied with currying favors with Whites that he is ready and eager to throw other Blacks under the bus. They look with a mixture of dismay and disgust as he becomes the celebrated token Black friend of Whites eager to show that they don't have a racial animus against *all* Blacks. *See? We're not racist. We like this Black guy! He's so refined! He's so cool! And he speaks French! Have you heard his accent? Why can't you guys be more like him?* African Americans watch this African play the role of model Black person, ingratiating himself with conservative Whites ecstatic at having found a Black person who validates their negative opinions of African Americans.

Father forgive him, for he knows not what he is doing. But someday, someone will call the cops on him or one of his loved ones, and he will begin to understand. Someday, he will have children, and they will not have his cool accent or his fancy French. And whatever they tell themselves about their identity, to the rest of the world, they will be Black first, and everything else second. And if he has a son, when that son becomes an adolescent, he will realize that society will start perceiving his boy as a threat. And when he is kept awake at night wondering how to keep his child from being shot by a cop who sees all Black boys as potentially violent criminals until proven otherwise, then he will understand what it means to be Black in America.

This is what I heard from African Americans. Not in words, but in an expressive gaze that it would take me years to understand. I deeply wanted to believe that racism was so absurd that it could not possibly persist in our world, and that whatever did continue was nothing more than vestigial remnants of a Jim Crow system that had only accidentally not been entirely dismantled. But they were right, and in time I would come to understand that for much of society, I would never be anything more than my complexion—a Black guy who just happens to have done some stuff. But in my early years in the US, I was so eager to distance myself from them and to show that I was a different sort of Black that every time someone referred to me as Black, I would reply, only half joking, "I'm not Black; I'm African."

CHAPTER 15

Speaking in Tongues

Maryland was proving to be less rosy than I had expected. My main talent, up to that point, had been getting good grades in school. But now, this was proving to be difficult. It was not that I was truly struggling, but I was finding it very hard to get As with anything like the ease I had been accustomed to. And I was at a loss over how to explain this development. Was my style different from what was required? Had my previous school been too easy? Was I letting my emotions get the better of me? I could never tell. Still, whatever it was, I knew I didn't like it, and I vowed to rectify the problem, if only I could diagnose it properly.

But school wasn't the only thing on my mind. There was also this matter of my new religion. Hamed was not just a Christian—he was a rather popular speaker in Pentecostal churches in and around Laurel. It helped that he had a compelling story to tell. His Eden was his life in Ivory Coast, the spoiled brat of a rich mother who catered to his every whim. He had spent his childhood traveling wherever he wanted, and had come to assume that this was the norm for everyone. But this paradise was lost when, after moving to the US to pursue his studies, he had a falling out with his mother. She responded by cutting off financial support and for the first time, he knew hunger. For the first time, he knew poverty. For the first time, he knew what it was like to sleep in a car during a cold American winter because you have nowhere else to stay. But in this moment of extreme vulnerability, when he had been abandoned by his own family, he found help and salvation in the embracing arms of the Church.

Yet for all his masterful oratory, for all his boasts of teaching computer science and having been hired by NASA to fix their computers, it was much easier to hear of Hamed's self-proclaimed accomplishments than to actually see them. The apartment he lived in was tiny. Cars that broke down went unfixed, ostensibly because he was a good mechanic and would get around to fixing them at some point. If you considered his claims with a skeptical eye, it was almost impossible to escape the conclusion that he wasn't earning much. It became apparent that he was staying afloat mostly thanks to the small but steady salary that his gentle and kind-hearted wife Jean—whom he terrorized with outbursts of anger—earned as a music teacher.

Hamed was the only child of Aunt Malon, one of my father's older sisters and the first daughter born to my paternal grandmother. She was a social worker and a college graduate at a time when the vast majority of women—if they attended school at all—stopped shortly after elementary school. Although she didn't earn much, she had a keen mind for investments, and over time amassed numerous rental properties around Abidjan. Much was expected of Hamed, being born to such a woman. And, it was true, he had been a good and perhaps even brilliant student in his youth, but had lacked the humility and patience to learn from anyone else. Whether through bad luck or self-sabotage, he had not fulfilled his promising potential. If a story were to be written about him, he would be a tragic hero who functioned more as a cautionary tale than a model worthy of emulation. This, at least, was the conclusion I reached.

And yet, this was the man who brought me to Christianity, although I'm not sure he realized what argument had convinced me. His was the kind of Church where the worship was full of all sorts of excitement. It was far removed from the Mass I had known in my 10 years of Catholic school, People threw themselves on their knees as they chanted. They loudly exclaimed their faith. They believed in demonic possession. The most characteristic feature of the church, however, was the ostentatious display of the gifts people had supposedly received from the Holy Ghost. Among these divine and ghostly gifts, the most prominent by far were the gift of tongues, and the gift of interpretation of tongues.

"And these signs shall follow them that believe; In my name shall they cast out devils; they shall speak with new tongues." This is what Christians believe that Mark said that Jesus said. And in the Pentecostal church my cousin introduced me to, these words had a literal meaning. "Tongues" was a language, or a mixture of languages. A careful listener observing those who received this gift would notice that the words were not actually forming meaningful sentences. What mattered more than the words themselves was the display of confidence and fervor with which they were uttered. They were delivered with an authoritative timbre, but the prosody was unlike that of any other language. Usually, the range of syllables was very narrow, so that it seemed that the same sounds were being repeated again and again.

Because speaking in tongues was seen as a favor from God, people who performed the act had special prestige within the community. But if you went to church for years and hadn't been favored by the Spirit enough to be able to speak in tongues, it indicated that perhaps you were not so pious. This gave everyone an incentive to try. I don't know how much of this I consciously thought while I attended this church. All I know is that there was something about the entire thing that left me uneasy. I had rejected Islam because I felt that it couldn't possibly be the word of God. But was this really the way God had chosen to bring salvation to humanity? There was another kid around my age in the church. Week after week, I noticed that he wasn't speaking in tongues. It seemed to me that he was also not given to theatrical displays of piety. I wanted to approach him. I had a question for him:

Hey, do you think they're making it up?

But I kept the question to myself, much as I wanted to have someone to talk to. I couldn't tell my parents about any of this. They might disown me if they learned that I had left Islam. And I couldn't tell anyone in this new community, for fear that I might be ostracized, and thereby lose both my Islamic and Pentecostal communities. What would be left to me, then? I resolved to keep my doubts to myself, and to do my best to keep on believing. I dove deep into my own mind, examining reasons for my discomfort, and realizing over time that my problem was not with

Islam, not with Christianity, but with the entire edifice of organized religion. All these things were so very obviously man-made. This was the most likely explanation for the mixture of hypocrisy and nonsensical rules I had observed within so many religious groups.

By the time I reached this conclusion, I was gone from Maryland. My mother had not fared well in Florida. She was returning to Michigan and asked if I wanted to return with her. After several months with Hamed, and realizing that no matter how dissatisfied I might be living with my parents, no one else would treat me any better, I jumped at the opportunity. I told Hamed that my mom wanted me to return to her. He was not happy with my decision, perhaps because he saw that he was losing along with my custody the ability to shape my mind. But he had already lost that battle. I was rapidly turning into my own man. Having discarded one religion in favor of another, it was going to be easier from now on to unshackle my mind from the ideas I had picked up when I was too young to form an independent judgment.

CHAPTER 16

Grizzly Beer

Back from Maryland, I returned to my high school in Michigan for my senior year. The first class I remember was English. The topic was *Beowulf*, which I frankly couldn't have cared less about. But after class, as usual, I lingered to talk to the teacher. I was reading *Phèdre*, a play by Jean Racine, a famous 17th-century French playwright. I told the teacher about him, and said that what impressed me most about French plays was that they were written from beginning to end in rhyming couplets. I added that even Shakespeare hadn't done that, feeling a sense of superiority about the French language similar to how people feel watching their national soccer team beat another. He informed me that Shakespeare had used some rhyming couplets in passages where he wanted to draw attention for a particular purpose. At the end of our short conversation, he told me that he thought I should be in honors English. I couldn't quite believe it. First of all, my English was terrible, and I wasn't sure how I would do in a regular English class. Second of all, I hadn't accomplished anything. All I had done was to have a short conversation about a play. Shouldn't honors be reserved for people who had proved themselves? And why was he assuming that I could write in English, solely on account of having talked to me about a *French* play? But I had a policy that I would never refuse to advance to a higher-level course, and it seemed cool to say that I had been able to reach an honors-level class merely a year after arriving. And so, I moved on to honors English.

I somehow survived. Here again, my luck served me well. It was rare that I had to write a whole essay from scratch on a topic that I had not previously known about. Sometimes, the teacher asked us to write only two paragraphs. Other times, we were told about the prompts in advance. In these instances, I made the most of my opportunity. I spent days mentally going over each sentence I would write and refining at least the first paragraph to my satisfaction. Again, the Latinate words were a great help. I would take a word in French, anglicize it, and hope that it would have the same meaning it had in French. This worked every single time, with the added benefit of giving my teachers the impression that I had a large vocabulary. Later in the semester, my teacher was impressed enough with me that she promoted me to AP English. Again, in spite of my diffidence, I accepted the promotion. My vanity would not let me pass up the opportunity to say that I had made it from non-fluency to AP English in a year and a half. At the end of my junior year, my English was still not great. I decided not to take the AP exam. The first reason was the problem of money. It cost $100 to sit for the exam, which seemed like a huge sum. The second was that I wasn't confident I could pass. But my teacher, Mrs. Mignon Hayes, believed in me. Not only did she encourage me to take the exam, but she actually paid for it herself. I took the exam and got a 3. It wasn't great, but it was enough to get college credit.

As my written English was improving, there was one thing that remained hard for me to grasp about my adoptive language: how in the world did people decide how a word should be pronounced? In French, the rules about how to pronounce combinations of letters can be daunting for newcomers, but they have the virtue of being consistent. If, for instance you learned that *eau* was pronounced *o*, you would know how to pronounce every single word that ended with that letter combination, and there wouldn't be any surprise. But in English, there was seemingly no pattern. The opportunities for publicly making a fool of yourself were endless. I'd discover a word like *awry* and pronounce it *AWE-ree* for years until I heard someone on the radio talk about something gone *uh-WRY*. I was familiar with the word *ear*, which rhymed with fear, dear, and rear. So, I thought I was in safe territory when I decided to talk about a grizzly bear. Only, what came out of my mouth wasn't grizzly *bair* but grizzly *beer*.

My conversation partner was puzzled. And I was puzzled that he was puzzled. How could a person grow up in America and never have heard of a grizzly beer?

"You've never heard of a grizzly beer?"

"Um, are you trying to say grizzly *BAIR?*"

"*BAIR!?* Are you sure it's not grizzly *beer?*"

But he was sure all right, and more to the point, he was right. I'm still not entirely convinced. English is stupid. I still think it should be grizzly beer and panda beer.

CHAPTER 17

Mr. C

If English and social studies classes demanded a lot of effort, math and science were a breeze. The terminology was virtually the same as what I was used to. In trigonometry, *sinus* had become sine. There wasn't much room for confusion there. At first, I was put in a basic physics class, where the work for the first couple of weeks consisted of learning about units of measurement and simple conversions. I couldn't believe this was high school. The teacher could see that I was bored out of my mind. She talked to the teacher next door. He was a young guy, in his mid-20s, who was teaching physics and AP Chemistry. She asked if he'd be willing to take me into his class. The class was full, but she talked him into it. It was the beginning of one of my longest-lasting friendships, with a man I still communicate with more days than not.

His name was Dave Consiglio. And his physics class was fun! It was one of my favorite times of the day. He was wicked smart, kinder than any teacher I'd ever had in Ivory Coast, and clearly interested in helping, which was great because I looked like a kid in need of help. My family was poor, *very* poor. My first winter in Michigan, I had a flimsy jacket that didn't offer much insulation against the cold. I wore the same clothes over and over again. And Mr.

C, as I called him at the time, was one of the few adults I could talk to about my life. I had heard others call me a nerd. I had never heard that term before and the concept was not something that had existed in Ivory Coast, where the kids with the highest grades had enjoyed the greatest amount of social prestige among their peers.

"Mr. C, do you think I'm a nerd?" I asked him once.

He didn't give me a direct answer. Instead, he told me that it was a good club to belong to.

Even the teacher thinks I'm a nerd, I thought. *I guess I must be a nerd.*

Insecure and awkward though I was, the idea that someone would mock me for being a good student was very irksome. And occasionally, I would fight fire with more fire: *So, you're laughing at me because I'm smarter than you?*

Needless to say, I was not very popular. But popularity wasn't what I was after. If you'd asked me what I wanted more than anything else, it would have been graduation, without hesitation. I liked my teachers more than I liked my peers. It seemed like the whole concept of adolescent rebellion was a waste of time. Most of the adults in front of me had presumably rebelled when they were teenagers. Yet there they were, going to work and definitely not being cool. Their rebellions must have failed, so why would mine be any more successful? Why not just buckle down, study, graduate, and get as good a job as I could? That seemed like a proposition much more likely to lead to success.

So I studied, and by the end of the first semester, I was promoted to AP Physics. I took and passed the AP Physics exam at the end of my junior year. Almost all my classmates were seniors. I watched them graduate, as I stayed behind. I couldn't help but feel that they were no more knowledgeable than I was, and that I should be allowed to graduate, too. There had been six years of elementary school in Ivory Coast, rather than the five that American kids undertook. I, too, had 12 years of education. Why couldn't I graduate with them? But there was nothing I could do.

The upshot of not graduating at 16 was that I got to spend an extra year with Dave Consiglio. This time, he was my AP Chemistry teacher. At the end of the year, I had the same problem I experienced with AP English—I didn't have the money for the exam fee. Mr. C, who had yet to become Dave for me, kindly gave me the money. I didn't do all that well on the exam, but I got a 3, enough to get college credit for the first semester of Chemistry. My mom was able to give me the money to take the AP Calculus exam, on which I scored a 4, giving me credit for the first two semesters of college calculus. I also took the AP French exam for good measure, feeling that it wouldn't hurt to have my foreign language requirement out of the way. Not surprisingly, I got a 5, the highest score possible.

CHAPTER 18

Culture Shock

The concept of nerdiness was a huge culture shock for me, but there were many other such things. For a kid who had moved from a land of scarcity to a land of plenty, the most striking of these was the pervasive waste of food. In Ivory Coast, even in rich families, the memory of poverty isn't that far off—either your parents grew up poor, or their parents grew up poor, or you have some poor aunts and uncles. There's a strong taboo against putting more on your plate than you can finish and throwing away the food you don't want instead of saving it for the next meal. But in America, every single day of high school I saw people casually throw away their lunch after taking only a few bites. That was hard to get used to, but by the end of high school, I had become so desensitized to it that I found myself doing the same.

There was also the fact that gay people were much more accepted. It was possible to be openly gay, and for it not to matter all that much. It was far from a paradise of perfect equality, but I had never met so many people so reluctant to engage in the gay bashing I had up to then taken for granted. The concept of gay rights didn't even exist where I grew up. Homosexuality wasn't viewed as a sexual orientation so much as sexual deviancy, a societal scourge that would lead to moral decay and societal collapse if it were tolerated. But here, people were gay and the sky wasn't dropping. It took me years before I could see that as normal.

A more annoying thing was the sheer depth of ignorance about all things African. When people weren't asking me idiotic questions about lions, they were betraying that they had no idea just how huge the African continent was. More than once, after telling people where I was from, I was asked if I was from South Africa. Even more irritating was being asked if I knew some guy from Tanzania. On the rare occasion when I sarcastically asked whether they knew some random guy from Mexico, no one understood what I was getting at. So, I would sigh to myself and change the topic of conversation.

American parenting was more intense than anything I had ever witnessed. Not only did parents seem indulgent in the extreme—simply accepting that it was in the nature of adolescents to talk back and be defiant—but they also seemed omnipresent. People would have a full-time job and then another full-time job attending the litany of things they enrolled their kids in: recitals, soccer games, hockey, baseball, summer camp. The last thing any kid back home had wanted was their parents showing up at a soccer game, loudly yelling words of encouragement. Oh the horror! Your friends would forever laugh at you for being a baby. The loss of prestige would be so immense that you'd never recover any shred of dignity. Parents might show up to big events, say, if you were a national finalist in some competition, but that was about it. But here, parents were everywhere, hovering like helicopters. It was mind-boggling!

There was also this matter of people hugging all the time. The culture I came from was decidedly not touchy feely. There was no "I love you" or "I miss you" among family members. Hugs were reserved for when someone was going on or coming back from a trip. I remember being nine years old and rushing to hug my mom, who had come to pick me up from school after being in the US for three months. Seeing her at my school was a huge surprise. But my friends were having none of it. I was a little baby for running to hug my mom, and that was that. But here, it seemed like everybody wanted a hug. At first, I would wonder, *what is wrong with this girl?* But after it kept happening, I realized that I was the odd one for not liking hugs. I'm a convert to hugging now, but it was definitely an acquired taste.

It also took a while to get used to how forthcoming people were with personal matters. You'd meet strangers on the bus and they would tell you that their dad was dying from cancer, or that their parents were getting divorced. I still can't get my mom to tell me exactly how my grandmother died. Where I grew up, people are protective of that kind of information, and almost no one discusses the details of their medical conditions. It was strange until I realized that sharing such details with a stranger could have no ramifications. After all, who would they tell? They didn't know you, and anyone they might tell also had no idea who you were. There was nothing to fear from divulging such things. In a way, I concluded, a stranger might be the perfect person to talk to when you want to bare your soul.

CHAPTER 19

Teachers

As a teenager, I didn't have much in the way of clothes. And when that first winter struck, it struck hard. All I had for protection was a really flimsy jacket, a woolen hat that covered my ears, and a pair of gloves that left my hands freezing if I spent more than 15 minutes outside. The best part of my situation was that I didn't realize quite how poor I was. And so, it came as a bit of a surprise when Ms. B-K, one of my ESL teachers, offered me some clothes out of the blue. She was a middle-aged, bespectacled, skinny woman who wore her blonde hair cropped. She was very kind-hearted, and was the type of devout Christian who might reprimand a student for using the name of God in vain. Her sister's husband had just died from a cancer of the tongue, and she thought I could use his clothes. There was a bit of everything: T-shirts, polos, shorts, and even underwear. She never told me why she chose me out of all her students, all of whom were every bit as foreign as I was, but I concluded that I must look a lot poorer than I had realized. Still, it was a welcome gift, and it gave me a wardrobe that I could not have acquired any other way.

Ms. Hagman also helped me. She didn't seem religious at all. She was a bit older than Ms. B-K and also wore her hair cropped, but it was all white rather than blonde. She was in her mid-to-late 50s and could recall being 18 when Kennedy was assassinated. In her younger days, she had spent seven years teaching English in Japan. She had no children, lived with her Republican mother, and was a fierce Democrat who didn't have anything good to say about President Bush. She taught social studies in ESL, and it is with her that I made my first forays into American history. She, too, could see that I was poor, so she would employ me to help grade the papers of some of her other classes. Sometimes, she also had me help out at her house, but I wondered whether she really needed my help or was employing me as an excuse to give me the money she knew I needed so much.

I was also fortunate to have Mrs. Hayes for an English teacher. At the time, I couldn't distinguish among American accents, and she appeared to me like a brown-haired, middle-aged White woman with an aquiline nose. One day, in class, she was talking about the civil rights movement and her experiences on the receiving end of racism, with what I understood to be an implication that she was Black. I was confused, having never encountered anyone who was that light-skinned but considered them-selves Black. I was not yet familiar with the history of the one-drop rule in America, but the idea that she could be considered Black by anyone seemed ludicrous. In Ivory Coast, people could be either Black, White, or mixed. And she was more light-skinned than any mixed person I'd ever met. Still, none of the other students batted an eye when she mentioned that she was Black. So, I was forced to concede that, for the purposes of life in the United States, she was considered Black, though I did not understand why or how. After the class I approached her and confessed that all this time, I had assumed that she was White. She laughed it off and called me a precious little child. I was not sure whether I had offended her, but I needn't have worried. At the end of my senior year, she still paid for me to take the AP English exam.

But the teacher who helped more than anyone else was Mr. C. He was only nine years older than me, and in his younger days, he had been, like me, a nerd with not much of a social life. And so, recognizing in me a younger, much more African, much less Italian version of himself, he befriended me. He was part teacher, part older brother, part sounding board as I worked my way towards a political philosophy. I could and did tell him about everything. He was the first openly non-religious person I had ever met, and the only one I was able to discuss my doubts with without fear of ridicule or judgment. He also arranged for the school to help me with a grant of $1,000 when I graduated. If someone had told me then that we would still be talking to each other on an almost daily basis 15 years after my graduation, I would have instantly believed it.

CHAPTER 20

Appeal

Meanwhile, at home, there were always two pervading issues we couldn't forget about, try as we might. The first was that we were very poor. About a month after my mom, sister, and I arrived in the US, my father joined us. The result was that there were now eight us of in Dimanche's two-bedroom apartment. My parents tried their best to get on their feet. This was difficult because of the language barrier. My mom felt comfortable speaking some English to other Africans, but a sort of mutism would set in when it came to speaking with Americans. She also wasn't used to American expressions. My father was like an educated Frenchman who had learned English once upon a time, but who found it difficult to converse in real time. The other issue was that our move to the US had been a huge gamble. All we had were visitor visas. My parents didn't have the legal right to work. In order to find employment, they had to find Ivorians who were willing to let them work with their Social Security number. This is a common way for undocumented immigrants to find work. The deal is that, in exchange for the risk the person with the legal status takes by allowing you to work with their papers, they get to keep part or all of the tax return money at the end of the year. My parents were working minimum-wage jobs, and much of the time, only one of them had a job. In the end, it took six months before they felt secure enough to move to a place of our own. And even then, we had to rely on the Salvation Army for much of our furniture.

The second overarching issue was Dimanche herself, who lorded over us. She was a social worker, and not very rich herself. We were thankful to her for hosting us, but there are always frustrations that creep up in such arrangements. My mom did the bulk of the cooking and we had to do much of the cleaning, of which there was a lot to do. Dimanche's younger kids were eight-year-old fraternal twins, a boy named Nyema and a girl named Nyemade. They have grown into very fine adults, but at the time, it seemed like they were constitutionally incapable of leaving anything clean. Anyone who has ever asked children that age to help will know the frustration of wondering whether it's worth it. You have to spend a lot of energy trying to get them to clean. And when they do, they do a sloppy job of it, so that you find yourself cleaning up after them. At this time, Dimanche's oldest son and I were 15, and it seemed to us that we were doing all that could reasonably be asked of us. We had other things to do, you know? Like, why are you always trying to interrupt our video game sessions to tell us to clean some stuff? It was, like, so unfair.

There was also my little sister, Sarrah, who is seven years my junior. What were her struggles at this time? I know that she was having a hard time with English, as we all were. She would constantly be asking us to translate what Dimanche was saying. But, truth be told, I was never really worried about her. I figured that by the time she graduated from high school, our family would have been on its feet for a long while.

Shortly after arriving, we found a lawyer in Southfield. He was a middle-aged, mild-mannered man with a kindly face. He helped us apply for political asylum. We didn't know it at the time, but it was going to be a protracted battle. I remember having to go for a hearing in Chicago. It was my first time in the city, and it didn't make a favorable impression, probably because it was winter, and the cold wind made me feel like I was being frozen all the way to my bones. It must have been 2002. We went to some federal building and my parents testified with the lawyer while I waited. Then we retraced our steps back home to Michigan. A while after that, we got our answer: asylum was denied and removal proceedings would be initiated. We could either return to Ivory Coast or appeal. By this time a civil war had started in Ivory Coast. The decision wasn't hard: we appealed.

CHAPTER 21

Rebellion

Upon becoming the president of Ivory Coast, Gbagbo immediately realized that if he were to keep power in the long term, he would have to enlarge his base of support. As his predecessors had done before him, he turned to the vast patronage system at his disposal to purchase a broad base of support. The corruption he had railed against before taking power was now embraced. The new regime, it turned out, would not be so different from what it had replaced. This story is familiar all over Africa, and it is the root of the disillusionment so many Africans feel about politics.

But soon, something else familiar to other Africans struck Ivory Coast: a rebellion. The year was 2002, and the country awoke one September morning to news that northern troops had mutinied and launched simultaneous attacks in several cities all over the country. Within a day, they had control of the northern half of the territory, and it seemed that the Gbagbo administration was doomed. But the loyalist armed forces prevailed in the south, and the country was soon split in half. During the first night of the rebellion, the regime in power used what it perceived as a golden opportunity to strike at its opponents. Former president Robert Guei was murdered after taking refuge in a cathedral. Ouattara's house was also attacked, but he found refuge in the French embassy.

A month after the start of hostilities, French troops intervened to separate the two sides. They were quickly denounced and accused of neocolonialism. To the rebels, the French had prevented their total victory. But for supporters of the president, the French were preventing them from reasserting national territorial integrity. In early 2003, a peace agreement was signed that displeased everybody. Gbagbo was to remain president until the next elections. A new government of national reconciliation was to be formed, with rebel leaders in cabinet positions.

Gbagbo agreed only reluctantly, and many in the rebel forces were still trying to topple him. Gradually, amid mutual recriminations, the two sides grew apart and the unity government collapsed. The president's rule became more authoritarian. Militia and death squads were unleashed to beat the opposition into submission. Reforms intended to make an election possible were blocked. In November 2004, a presidential bomber attacked a French position, killing nine peacekeepers and wounding 31. The government claimed the attack was a simple mistake. But French president Jacques Chirac rejected this explanation and ordered a retaliation, which destroyed the entire Ivorian air force in the process. Gbagbo's wings had been clipped, at last, or so it seemed.

The French didn't realize how vulnerable they were to further escalation. At that time, there were around 8,000 French expatriates living in Ivory Coast. The president unleashed his supporters, and the French government was caught off-guard when thousands of French civilians in Abidjan were harassed by youth militia groups calling themselves Young Patriots. Huge riots targeted French schools and the French military base in Abidjan, long a symbol of imperialism to many Ivorians. France was drawn further into the conflict, sending in troops that spent days trying to quash the riots and airlift their citizens out. In the aftermath, most of the large French community was evacuated. On the international stage, it made ugly optics for French troops to put down rioters in an ostensibly independent country. It constituted a victory for Gbagbo, who for many on the continent became a courageous leader standing up to imperialists.

⊞

Where did the rebellion come from? For some, it was a spontaneous uprising of marginalized northern troops, who were simply demanding the end of second-class citizenship. But this, of course, doesn't explain where the funding and training for such a massive uprising came from. For others, it is certain that Burkina Faso's fingerprints were all over the operation, many of the rebels having trained there. This is highly probable, and there is a long history of African leaders funding rebellions in other countries. Aside from this, it was common knowledge that the biggest beneficiary of this rebellion would be Ouattara. How plausible was it that his hands could be entirely clean?

Holding high political office in an African nation is a very attractive proposition, given the lack of meaningful restrictions on power. What's more, political power in many African states remains the surest path to wealth. Groups that are locked out of power can also be locked out of wealth acquisition, often for decades. The rewards being so high, politicians will often take whatever aid is offered, financial or military, foreign or domestic, in order to attain their goal. Much of the time, many ethnic groups outside of power can point to a long list of injustices from the authorities. So, when rebellions arise, they are often supported by a large portion of the population. It's a cynical game that is possible because in such young nations, attachment to an ethnic group is often stronger than attachment to the country.

CHAPTER 22

Cruel Joke

There was never enough money. When I had to ask my mom for $100 to pay for a TI-83 calculator, I felt like the worst sort of child. How dare I ask her to spend such a sum while we were barely making ends meet? It was only with gifts from the Salvation Army that we were able to get established once we left Dimanche's apartment. They gave us living room furniture and even a desktop computer. I was ecstatic. My mom went grocery shopping at places like Aldi and Save A Lot. And towards the end of each month, I could overhear my parents wonder how they could possibly pay both the rent and the bills.

These were the issues I was wrestling with as I went to school. At home, there was a very stressful environment, with the twin pressures of our poverty and uncertain immigration status taking their toll on us. My father, who had never been easy to live with, was finding constant fault with me. It seemed like there was nothing I could do to avoid his displeasure. On one occasion, my parents tried to pressure me into finding a job so that I could contribute to the family's expenses. They would point to the children of other African immigrants. Such and such is working. This other child has a job. Why did I think that it was okay to sit at home doing nothing to help? I resisted their pressure. Those other kids didn't have the grades I had. It seemed to me that their parents were jeopardizing their futures by asking them to divert their energies into menial jobs rather than to their studies. I would have none of it. My future was in academics. This was where my talents lay. The idea that I should work, to the possible detriment of my grades, seemed like short-term gain for long-term pain.

Thankfully, they didn't insist, and I was able to continue to devote myself to school. But, during my senior year, there was the problem of applying to college. Ms. B-K had once asked me whether I would go to college. I had been so surprised by the question that I hadn't been sure what she had meant. I had never considered for an instant the idea of *not* going to college. But now that it was time to apply, I had to consider the matter of my political status. All of the application forms asked if you were a citizen, a permanent resident, or a holder of a foreign student visa. My political status, after appealing the asylum denial, was "pending." I froze every time I got to this section. My counselor wasn't very helpful. Perhaps he was overworked. It seemed to me that he didn't have very much time to devote to each student. He merely told me to fill out the applications as best I could. I couldn't turn to my parents, because they understood even less about the American university system than I did. I had good grades. My test scores had been decent. If memory serves, my ACT score was a 25, but I'd only been in the country for about six months. I took the SAT six months later and scored 1310/1600.

Still, it seemed to me that I was simply ineligible for admission to a university. So I was gripped by paralysis as the application deadlines passed me by. In those days, there was an exam called the Michigan Educational Assessment Program or MEAP. Students who did well on it would receive a $2,500 scholarship. This should have been enough money to pay for at least a semester's worth of tuition at an in-state school. But I was not considered a legal resident of the state of Michigan, even though I resided there. And so, in addition to the normal tuition and fees, I would have to pay the exorbitant out-of-state differential fee. With these expenses, the only place I could afford tuition was a community college. But even that was expensive. I was charged a higher rate because we were neither residents in Michigan nor property owners in Oakland County. That last one in particular seemed like a cruel joke. People at the college thought they were making a helpful suggestion when they asked if my parents had considered owning property in the county. I was dirt poor, and so were my parents. This was like telling someone my car had broken down and being asked why I didn't drive the spare Mercedes. Still, I had enough to pay for a semester's worth of classes at Oakland Community College. I enrolled for a semester and hoped that things would somehow work out.

CHAPTER 23

June

Oakland Community College in Farmington Hills, Michigan, seemed to have the most beautiful campus in the world. This was for the simple reason that I had seen no other campus when I started classes there in the fall of 2003. In retrospect, I'm hard-pressed to say what I loved so much about it, save that the lawns were very well manicured. To my 17-year-old eyes, it also seemed to have the most beautiful girls in the entire world, but I was exceedingly awkward with women and couldn't imagine why any of them would want to date me. I was very conscious of the fact that I had no social skills. It appeared that I was younger than every single person on campus. And my conversational English was still not all that great. It was hopeless.

My favorite subject in high school had been math. "I don't know what course others may take, but as for me, give me calculus or give me death." I had learned about Patrick Henry's speech and, thinking myself exceedingly clever, taken to writing my version of it on blackboards after class. It was no accident that I was seen as a very, very odd duck. But high school was gone. And I had to decide what exactly I wanted to study. I had liked math and physics, and therefore told myself that I would like engineering. It seemed to make sense. My hardest class that first semester was Calc III, but I enjoyed it very much. I also liked my history class, which was taught by a man who in retrospect was an eccentric amalgam of conservative and Black nationalist. He found such unlikely things as Tecumseh's curse plausible. Nevertheless, I very much enjoyed his lectures, especially because we were both admirers of Alexander Hamilton.

Hamilton was the hero that I needed. He was the wunderkind who had immigrated to the colonies as a teenager and overcome much adversity to become one of the greatest and most important founding fathers. He was the man I wanted to be. Because his favorite poet was Alexander Pope, I tried to read Alexander Pope. Because he had read Hume, I tried to read Hume. Because his prose was complex and hard to understand, I tried to make my prose—even emails—hard to understand, in the mistaken belief that opaqueness of meaning was a reflection of intelligence. It goes without saying that his enemies became my enemies, and there is no one I hated more than Thomas Jefferson, the slave owner who had written that Blacks were "inferior to the whites in the endowments both of body and mind." I devoured biographies of Hamilton, which in retrospect had all been written more as hagiographies than as scholarly attempts to explain the man in his historical context. I came away from these books genuinely puzzled that anyone might find anything admirable about Jefferson.

But it wasn't the classes I was taking that would change my life. I was fortunate to be assigned June

Swartz as my counselor. The first thing she noticed about me was my transcript. The five AP exams I had taken in high school had given me 34 college credits at OCC. She wasn't used to seeing such records. She looked at me with a puzzled expression.

"What are you doing *here*?"

I sighed. I talked about being an undocumented immigrant, with a political status that was "pending," a word that made me feel that a sword of Damocles was hanging over my head, ready to fall any moment. I talked about my application for asylum having been initially denied, and about having a lawyer who had appealed the case. I talked about my hopes and ambition, and the thick cloud of uncertainty hanging over them. She listened, alternately nodding and shaking her head. She was going to see what she could do, she said. I didn't know what to expect, but I didn't want to hope for too much and set myself up for disappointment.

Before the end of my first semester, my family received an update on our appeal: it had been denied. I was crestfallen. Up to then, I had kept hope, and perhaps even an expectation, that the immigration issue would be resolved in our favor. But now, what was there to do? The lawyer said we should appeal again. We didn't have much to lose. So, we appealed again. But that wasn't going to help me with school in the meantime. I was ineligible for financial aid, and even loans. Nor was I eligible for most scholarships. Since our case was still in court, we had been granted Social Security cards and work authorization permits. But there was only so much money I could bring in with my lowly jobs. What to do? What to do?

This is when I decided to pursue a degree in nursing. My plan was to ditch engineering and start taking nursing prerequisites. Then I could apply for admission to an associate degree in nursing, then enroll in a bachelor's degree program. Once employed as a nurse, I could see if my employer would sponsor me for permanent residency, or whether I could emigrate to another Western nation such as Canada or Australia. I would later learn that this plan had a very scant chance of success, but this was the best my 17-year-old brain could up with. I had to try something, and this was something, so I thought I had nothing to lose. All things considered, it was better than sitting around waiting for a *deus ex machina* rescue from my woes.

But there was still the matter of paying for the second semester of school. One of the advantages of having a large extended family is you might have a successful relative with the means to help you out financially. In my case, that relative was Uncle Mory. He was my father's older brother by three years, and had obtained a law degree in France after working for a few years there as a hospital orderly. He had returned to Ivory Coast and been quite successful as a lawyer. Fond of motorcycles, and often seen sporting an expensive hat, he had a reputation as a bon vivant, and it was he who convinced me to go to medical school. His pitch was basically that work was not meant to be a matter of passion, but one of hard-headed analysis. I had told him that I was not sure what I wanted to do after my nursing degree. Med school was long and hard, and I wasn't sure that I had the passion and dedication to make it work. I was thinking of law school, healthcare administration, or even physics, I told him. He told me that, like me, he had many intellectual interests. But among these, only the law could have allowed him to earn enough to have the lifestyle he wanted.

"Sometimes I have to wake up early in the morning to go defend a thief. Do you think I sent him to steal?"

It was a rhetorical question, but he let it hang there for a few seconds, as though he expected a response. At last, I shook my head. He continued, adding that he did it because it was what paid the bills. He gave me examples of friends of his who had studied things they were more passionate about, only to have to ask him for money later on. He also told me that he had given a few older cousins of mine the same advice, which had been ignored. They had pursued degrees in marketing or communications, only to find after graduating that it was not so easy to land a good job.

"What about being a lawyer? You've done it! And it's worked quite well for you."

"The career of a lawyer is subject to too many aleatory things. I earn a good living, but I often have to be up preparing for a case long into the night. Try to find a job that doesn't follow you home when you leave for the night."

Aleatory! What a word! *Alea iacta est*, Caesar had supposedly said: the die is cast. What Uncle Mory was saying was that the practice of law was subject to too many random factors that could affect success or failure. Medicine was a more stable choice. He didn't seem to realize that this is also a career in which the job follows you home. In any case, I let his advice play in my head over the next few months. For a young man who feared having to struggle to find a good job after graduating, it was sound advice.

I decided that, unlike some of my older cousins, I would listen to my uncle. Still, for the time being, my priority was to find a way to pay for school.

I was still living with my parents and sister during my first year of college. One night, during dinner, my father said that he had news for us. News? My mom and I looked at him expectantly, hoping that it was something good. It was indeed. Uncle Mory had sent us a gift of $4,000. This was a game changer, and about $2,500 of the money promptly went to my tuition. After peering deeply into the uncertainty and darkness that lay before us, we had a bit of respite from our financial difficulties.

I did well in my pre-nursing classes and at the end of the semester, June wanted to see me. I wasn't sure what it could be about. Was she going to tell me that my situation was hopeless? That seemed like the most likely scenario. It was not a meeting I was looking forward to. I had no idea what I was going to do. I had started community college with an understanding that I would figure it out as I went. And now, it seemed like I wasn't going to be able to figure it out after all.

CHAPTER 24

The Shadow of God

Long before the Supreme Court legalized gay marriage in the US, I had become a fierce supporter of the idea. It had not always been this way. I had started out as a homophobe, then morphed into someone who thought the idea of gay marriage was comical. But I listened to argument after argument for why it should not be allowed and felt that, at the end of the day, they were all grounded in the idea that gay people were somehow less moral than the rest of us, and that their relationships were therefore less worthy of respect. I realized that the anti-gay marriage tribe was no longer mine. I didn't like to feel that I was on the side of oppression and hatred. I hadn't thought of myself as an ally of the queer crowd before, and I had expressed surprise when, in nursing school, I had seen one of my classmates attach a gay pride flag to the rearview mirror of her car. But the gay marriage debate had forced me to pick a side, and more than anything else, it was the arguments advanced by one side that had convinced me to join the other.

A similar process occurred with my religious views. After returning to Michigan from Maryland, I quickly realized that I no longer believed that Jesus was the son of God. All it had taken was a bit of space and time to myself to allow me to reach my own conclusions. I had also been swayed by believers, whose arguments I found exceedingly wanting. Every time one of them opened his mouth to explain that Jesus was divine because the Bible said so, and that the Bible was the inerrant word of God, I realized that I was not a Christian. Every time someone expressed certainty in creation, or opposition to evolution, or a conviction about what it took to get into heaven, I knew I no longer believed in these ideas. Every time someone told me of original sin, or of Adam and Eve, I wanted to roll my eyes. After several months of this, I wasn't sure exactly what I believed in, but I knew for sure what I didn't believe in.

All major religions seemed to me to contain some obvious mythology, which was recognizable as such to everyone but their own followers. And yet, it also seemed that these religions, flawed as they were, were repositories of great wisdom. And so, at age 17, I came up with a worldview that reconciled these conflicting feelings of mine. I had learned about Plato's allegory of the cave, and this was my inspiration for my understanding of God. My God was like a man standing under the sun, his shadow cast across the floor. Around this shadow were different groups of people who could not see the man. All they saw was a two-dimensional representation, which they mistook for him. What was more, they were seeing different facets of him, here a hand, there a foot, here the torso, there the legs, here the head, there an elbow. Each of them could see only pieces of the puzzle, and all of them, though they were correct in their understanding of the part that lay in front of them, could not grasp his true nature. They could not see the white of his eyes. They could not see that his nose and ears were made of cartilage. And they could not see that he had a heart, which pumped blood full of red cells, which in turn were packed with hemoglobin, and this hemoglobin had molecules of oxygen attached, oxygen which would be transported to every organ and every tissue of his body, keeping him alive. Every time they wanted something, they prayed to the part of the man they saw. And every time they obtained something they wanted after praying, they ascribed it to the hand god, or the foot god, or whatever interpretation of whatever shadow or whatever body part they had been taught to see. But in the end the man was just there, existing, but not at all concerned with intervening in their affairs.

This was a god I could believe in, a god who was both more and less than the one I had grown up with. He was more of a god than my previous God because he transcended religion and dogma. But he was also less than the God I grew up worshiping, because he was unavailable to answer prayers or offer comfort and solace in times of hardship. This god was tailor-made for me, because he was, in the end, my own creation. And yet, though he fully satisfied me on an intellectual level, I soon found out that it is almost impossible to worship such a god. For what, after all, is the point of praying to a god who does not listen and will not help? And how exactly does it differ, if at all, from talking to yourself? I did not have much of an answer. Or perhaps I did have an answer, but an answer I dared not utter aloud. Perhaps I had created this creator because the rest of religion no longer made any sense, and this god whose touch was so light that it might as well not exist was the only thing I had to hang on to if I wanted to say that I still believed in God. After all, what kind of reprobate and fool would reject the obvious and undeniable existence of God? Not me, definitely not me.

CHAPTER 25

Nursing School

When I got to my appointment with June, she had an affability I didn't know how to read. Was she just going to let me down easy? I braced myself for the worst as we exchanged pleasantries. But then, to my surprise, she told me something I had not dared to dream of—she had found me a scholarship to attend Eastern Michigan University. It turned out that she had some connections at the school from her days as a high school counselor. After hearing my story, the university had decided to grant me a scholarship that would pay the out-of-state differential in full. Now, all my family would have to do is come up with the cost of tuition. This was still a lot of money, to be sure, and I still had no idea how I would find it. But that was a bridge I would cross when I got there. To say that I was elated would be a huge understatement. In spite of all this, I wasn't yet out the woods. If I wanted to be able to attend nursing school, I was going to have to work a lot over the summer.

I didn't have a summer break that year. Instead, I used the time to complete my prerequisites. Officially, the nursing school at EMU accepted only 80 students per year. But they reserved the right to make exceptions. The year before my admission, 12 extra students had been admitted. So, the fact that the school had decided to admit me even though I had applied relatively late was not entirely unusual, especially given that I had a 3.97 GPA. Among the classes that I took that summer was a survey of organic and biochemistry. This was a one-semester course, rather than the two-semester course pre-med students take. It gave me the mistaken impression that that organic chemistry was an easy subject. Another class was Human Growth and Development. This was the first in a long series of classes in which I would learn about childhood developmental milestones, the bane of my existence. There are some subjects that come naturally, others that you can grasp with some effort, and still others that you can never remember, no matter how many times you try to learn them. To me, remembering what a child is supposed to be able to do at various ages and when certain reflexes are supposed to disappear will always be an example of the last type of subject. Pediatrics was apparently not for me.

I was one of only four men in my nursing class. And, at 18, I was the youngest in the class. Nursing was very popular among people looking for a second career. Students like me, who had entered nursing school a year after graduating from high school, were in the minority. But I was not intimidated. In fact, I felt rather cocky as school started. I had aced my third-semester calculus class. How hard could this possibly be? It could be quite challenging, in fact, and for a reason I had not anticipated. I had always loved math and had always been interested in most of my classes. In my sociology class at OCC, I had frequently read textbook chapters. But my marriage with nursing was not born out of love; it was a marriage of convenience. Lucky though I was to have been accepted to this school so many struggled to enter, I was viewing it as nothing more than a stepping stone. And so studying proved harder than it had ever been. I also had no hospital experience. And although I could study pathophysiology as well as anyone else, questions about what to do in a given situation always left me baffled.

The school felt very cliquish and I didn't have very many friends. My main friend was Michaele, who happened to be renting a room in the same rooming house where I was staying. It was an old house right across the street from campus. The rent was cheap at $250 a month, but you got what you paid for. The landlord was a man in his 70s named Alan. He loved to bark at people. The place was very cold during the winter, which was torture for me. If there is one thing I hate, it is winter. If there one thing I hate even more, it's a poorly heated home in winter. What's more, Alan was deathly afraid of space heaters, seeing them as a fire hazard. I had a room downstairs that opened onto the small kitchen. The fridge was also small, and there wouldn't have been enough room for the food of five tenants, except that I couldn't afford to buy much, and my housemates rarely cooked. There was a creaky stairway that led upstairs, where there were two bedrooms and the sole bathroom of the house, an arrangement that left me with a lifelong distaste of sharing my bathroom. I usually called Michaele by her last name, Bannow, probably because it felt weird to call a girl *Michael,* as her name was pronounced. She was something of an older sister to me, with a streak for playing practical jokes. On one occasion, she and her boyfriend came into the house dressed as crash dummies, a term I didn't have in my vocabulary. I was in the kitchen when they came home and they just stood at the door, staring at me. I had no idea who they were. I looked at them, scared, but trying to put on a brave face. I thought of asking them if they wanted to share my meal, as a way to break the ice and release the tension I was feeling, but all I found myself voicing was a long, interrogative "*huh?*" After about a minute of staring me down, they turned and left, leaving me wondering whether I had just dreamed the entire encounter. Thinking myself in safe company, and that I had successfully hidden my fear, I confessed to Michaele what had happened, only to see her laugh hysterically and confess that it had been her. I had been played.

I also became friends with Melissa, whom my mom really liked. She was the classmate who had the gay pride flag on her rearview mirror. Melissa had gotten pregnant at 16 but refused to let herself be slowed down. She was smart, funny, and short—but then again, I thought everyone was short. She was no longer with her daughter's father, but was married to a computer nerd whose main activities, as best I could tell, were playing video games and drinking beer. When my mom met her, she mentioned Julien Clerc's song *Mélissa.* I'm pretty sure my mom hadn't been aware that the lyrics were about Peeping Toms spying on a woman named Melissa as she repeatedly tried to shoo them away. I found myself translating those lyrics to Melissa during one of our car rides to our clinicals. She thought it was the funniest thing in the world—not the actual lyrics, but that my mom would have mentioned this song upon meeting her.

Besides Michaele and Melissa, I had many other acquaintances in nursing school. There were Ashley and Emmy, the inseparable twins, who were not actually twins but never seemed to be without one another. The first was a tall brunette—I guess I lied when I said that I thought everybody was short. She was ambitious and seemed to have decided that she was going to marry rich, and soon. She had the looks to pull it off and did just that about a year into nursing school. Emmy was small-framed, short, blue-eyed, and blonde. During my first clinical, I asked her the dumbest question I have ever heard anyone ask aloud. My instructor had told me to flush a patient's intravenous line. I didn't know where to get a syringe, and I was deathly afraid to ask. I was in the position of a dangerous ignoramus whose primary instinct was hiding the depth of his ignorance. But I had enough sense to ask a classmate.

"Hey, where do I get those syringes?"

"In the supply room."

"The instructor asked me to flush his IV. What do I flush it with, just water?"

"No, with saline."

"Oh, right."

To her credit, Emmy didn't mock me. In fact, she did nothing at all to make me feel like the idiot I knew I was. Later, it dawned on me that water was both hypotonic and not sterile.

Oh my God, I thought, *I hope I don't do something really, really stupid. I'd better make sure I double check everything with people, even if I'm afraid to ask my instructor.* And so, for the remainder of my clinical years, I asked my colleagues anything I wasn't sure about, especially when the instructor was intimidating.

I was also friends with Michael, a veteran who was 10 years older than me. He was a bit too old and had seen too much for me to consider him a peer. He had an opinion on everything, and it was hard to disagree with him without feeling like an idiot. He was driven, super confident, and popular with classmates and teachers alike. There was also Brad, who seemed way too cool for me. Alongside the nursing curriculum, he was also taking pre-med classes. Like me, he had thoughts of going to med school someday. And finally, there was Josh, who stood at an impressive 6'5" and who had a wealth of stories to tell. He had gone to an evangelical Christian school, but had moved away from religion after reading the Bible cover to cover. His first college major had been history, and he had absorbed what seemed like an encyclopedic knowledge of various Native American tribes. Dropping out from his history program after a couple of years, he had taken a job in a warehouse earning $12 an hour. But he wanted something more and decided to pursue nursing, which was a career that promised stable employment and several different paths to advancement. There were many true believers in nursing school—people who had taken to heart the Gospel of Nursing, which preaches that nursing is the greatest of careers, and that it is nurses who *truly* run hospitals and train physicians. This school of thought teaches that, unlike physicians, who stay far away doing God knows what, nurses *really* care and are at the patient's bedside doing the most important job in the hospital. It was impossible to stay in nursing school for several years without absorbing a version of this attitude to some degree. But Josh was decidedly not a true believer. Not surprisingly, he was one of my closest friends, and still is to this day.

A curious development occurred after my admission to nursing school. I kept waiting for a bill that never came. The scholarship I had received was supposed to pay the out-of-state differential and I was supposed to be charged out-of-state tuition. But the school made a mistake, and I was charged in-state tuition. The result was that it looked as though the school owed me money, since the out-of-state differential was by far the higher value. For a time, I wondered whether they would catch their mistake. I waited, and waited, and waited, but nothing happened. It was definitely not something I was going to complain about. If the school wanted to charge me in-state tuition, who was I to tell them to do otherwise? Finally, after several months, used to the idea that I would not be charged any tuition, I began to wonder whether the school would actually issue me a refund. It was a preposterous idea, to be sure, but what seemed even more ridiculous was the idea that I should complain about it, should it happen. It never did. But at the end of the year, the school caught their mistake.

My heart sank. I knew that if they asked me to pay the entire bill, I would be ruined. My family was still poor. My mom was a nursing assistant at a group home and my dad delivered mail. There was no way either of them would have been able to contribute much to my tuition. But again, my seemingly limitless good fortune smiled on me. The school should have told me that I owed money. Or, if they judged that I had not been at fault for their mistake in the first year's tuition, they should at least have said that they would charge me out-of-state tuition going forward. But they chose neither of those options. Instead, I was told that since I was being charged in-state tuition, I was no longer eligible for the scholarship I had been receiving, and I would get another scholarship instead. This scholarship would, of course, be smaller than my previous one, but the overall effect of these changes was a marked reduction in the amount I was supposed to pay each year. True, my parents would have to help me with some of the tuition, and this would still demand a huge percentage of their meager resources, but I could not lose sight of the fact that although I was basically an undocumented immigrant, I had been admitted to a competitive nursing program and had received a whole year of free tuition. This remains, to this day, one of the luckiest breaks I've ever gotten. It is the cumulative effect of many such lucky breaks that makes the difference between sinking and staying afloat.

CHAPTER 26

Unsteady

Like many children who have been in the same situation, when my parents were estranged from one another, I was forced to contemplate choosing between them. The idea of making a choice didn't really bother me, but the idea of proclaiming that choice aloud did. As an adult, I also didn't want to have to choose, but this time it was between godliness and godlessness. I had been raised with the faith of the crescent, but I had seen my faith crack like a fragile eggshell the first time I had submitted it to a test. And so, I had put aside the crescent and picked up the cross. But it, too, cracked, and I found myself having to create a new faith from scratch. After standing in front of the canvas for months, I had decided that what suited me best was a blank canvas, a metaphor for the mystery I understood God to be. But then, much to my surprise and annoyance, I noticed the blank canvas cracking.

I had preached my version of God to only a few people, but I had preached to no one as much as I had preached to myself. I had tried to make myself a convert to the new faith I had created, but I had failed. Every time I tried to explain this God I believed in, I sounded irrational to myself. I was using a lot of words, but they amounted to nothing more than poetry. There was no substance there and I knew it. And so, after a couple of years of this neo-deism, I had come to the realization that, though I could not say that I disbelieved—I did not, could not, disbelieve—it was also evident that I no longer believed. What was I then? This is when I discovered agnosticism, and it seemed to be an answer to all my questions.

Agnosticism was an acknowledgment of my lack of *gnosis*, my lack of knowledge. It was a brilliant solution. I could just admit aloud that I did not know whether there was a God, and this would enable me to avoid taking a position. The form of agnosticism I found most appealing was strong agnosticism, which posits that the existence of God is not only unknown, but that it is fundamentally unknowable. This was faith not only in the unknown, but in unknowability itself. It was a commitment to being noncommittal, which was precisely what I needed at the time. Faced with an unwanted choice between God and no God, my will had torn itself into so many pieces that it had melted. Agnosticism was the receptacle that could receive this molten will and give it shape and substance anew.

And there I stayed, ensconced in my position, from which vantage point I could rain condescension at will onto believers and deniers alike. They seemed to me to be two sides of the same pretentious coin, two similar types of unfounded faith. Paradoxically and oxymoronically, I took a certain sense of pride in my humility, which enabled me to acknowledge that I simply did not know. I was like one of those political centrists who takes great pleasure in criticizing and deriding the perceived excesses of both left and right, and who incessantly pontificates to anyone willing to listen their views of how much better the world would be if only it could be remade in the image of centrism.

But there was a certain vulnerability in my position. I had not adopted it out of conviction, but out of fear—a fear I refused to face, the fear of what my own heart contained. It is almost impossible to be agnostic and to assign an equal probability to the existence or non-existence of God. And many agnostics, if they are honest with themselves, will acknowledge that their position is much closer to atheism than it is to theism. That is, if they are given only the choice of picking the more likely scenario—God or no God—they will almost invariably choose the latter, especially if the God in question is clad in the trappings of a specific religious tradition. Perhaps not all agnostics feel this way. But I certainly did. And because I did, I was like an unsteady man ready to fall at the slightest shove.

CHAPTER 27

Samurai

I was not very close to my father as a child, and to this day I feel much closer to my mom. The observant reader will not fail to notice that in the previous sentence, I contrasted *mom* with *father*, not with *dad*. This is a consequence of their different parenting styles. My father had a habit of explicitly stating to his children that he was not their friend. It seemed that he had only three things to impart: discipline, advice, and money. This is a style of parenting in which the father is a powerful and emotionally distant, almost divine, figure to whom children owe reverence and devotion. The problem with it is that when the children grow and no longer want nor need discipline from their parent, there isn't much that remains to the relationship.

Even as a teenager, I had a rather strong paternal instinct. When I turned 20, dreaming of a father I could connect with and relate to, I imagined that it would be nice to meet the 20-year-old version of my father. Would we be friends? What would we talk about? Would he tell me about his hopes and dreams, his fears and stressors? Would it be easier to connect with him as a young man? Expecting that I would be a father myself someday, I undertook to do for my children what my I wished my father had done for me: I would trap the soul of my 20-year-old self in the pages of a journal. I was not as frequent a writer as I would have liked. There always seemed to be something more important to do than write in this journal, and in the end, it took me eight years to fill it up. But I did write some interesting entries, such as one from February 8, 2008.

I grew up watching anime in Ivory Coast. Anime had been popular in France and so in the 1980s, lots of Japanese anime had been dubbed into French. My favorites were the kind that featured lots of fighting, especially shows that were samurai-themed. It was not very surprising, then, that when *The Last Samurai* came out in 2003, I fell in love. I imagined that maybe I, too, could be a samurai. I even went so far as to purchase wooden training swords, in the expectation—never realized—that I would play at sword fighting with a dear friend of mine. Unable to do with these swords what I dreamed of doing, I resolved to do the next best thing: I walked around my university campus with my sword at my side.

Today, I know better than to walk around carrying a sword, wooden or otherwise. But as a shy, diffident, 20-year-old anime nerd, the furthest thing from my mind was that anyone would be scared of *me*. So, one night, I decided I was a samurai, dammit. And what was the point of being a samurai if you couldn't walk around with your sword, hitting the occasional defenseless tree branch? I made my way to a small, independent drug store to purchase some rubbing alcohol or whatever else I needed that night. I was very polite and it didn't occur to me that anyone might have been uncomfortable, especially given that I had made sure to hand them the sword when I entered.

I had also passed a few members of the Student Eyes and Ears for University Safety on my way there, without incident. Someone on the street had told me to "be careful with that," but I hadn't made much of it. After leaving the store, I went to sit in the dark on one of the benches on campus, lost in the immense sea of my own thoughts.

From the darkness, I noticed the fiery, yellow, reptilian headlights of a university police car some distance away. Unconcerned, unperturbed, and unable to imagine that I could be its intended prey, I returned to my thoughts, only to realize a few minutes later that the reptile I had thought far away had stealthily slinked its way towards me. The headlights, brighter than ever and now only a few yards away, pulled me out of my reverie. Slowly an officer climbed out of the car and walked towards me. For a few seconds that felt like an eternity, we looked at each other. Then he broke the silence and asked to see my sword. Smartass that I was, my first thought was to tell him that I presumed he could see my sword, since he was not blind, but I thought better of it. Next, I had the thought of getting down on one knee, and presenting the sword to him with my palms up, as though I were re-enacting some ritualistic sword presentation ceremony, but I thought better of that too. And here, my journal entry and my rec-ollections diverge. I recall the police officer telling me that he had heard reports of a guy going around with a sword, and he had me hold my hands in the air at gunpoint while telling me to set the sword aside. In my journal entry, I wrote that he asked me to hold my hands up, and that I felt that I could die if I made one wrong step or moved too fast, but I wrote nothing about the gun. Whichever of these is true, he inspected the sword, gave it back to me, checked my ID against a database, and told me to do him a favor by taking it home and not taking it out with me again. That was my most direct encounter with a police officer. I was not eager to repeat the process. I did as he had instructed, and no one ever saw the sword again.

CHAPTER 28

Arabic Lesson

I had many roommates while I was living at Alan's rooming house. There was Wanda, an old lady who constantly
harassed me about what I felt were inconsequential
things, and to whom I finally left a very nasty letter, the
content of which I have since forgotten. There was my
friend Michaele, who left the house after about a year.
There was Luanne, who was 39 years old and from Adrian,
Michigan—which she disliked immensely—and with
whom I had many conversations long after I was supposed
to go to bed. There was also Al Anud, a Muslim Koweiti
woman to whom I somehow felt free to reveal my irreligiosity. I was relieved to find that she was more amused
than offended. But among the most memorable of the lot,
there was Muhammad, an exchange student from Saudi
Arabia, who, as best I could tell, was a devout Muslim.

Muhammad didn't have any female friends, which
I attributed to his religiosity. Seeing that he had trouble
making friends, I proposed to introduce him to Josh, but
he declined, stating that he only liked Black men. I was a
bit taken aback, but I thought that maybe he very strongly
identified with the civil rights movement and had developed undue animosity towards Whites. But there was
another explanation, which I learned when Muhammad

brought a friend home. Another housemate told me that he had seen them come out of the shower together. This was peculiar, I thought, but it was none of my business. It still seemed odd to me that someone so very Muslim could be gay, but I figured that he must be finding the US liberating after leaving his very conservative country.

At some point, Muhammad very excitedly told me that he was going to Gaylord, Michigan. The school offered a winter program there, and he seemed very eager to go. What he did not say but hinted at was that he hoped that Gaylord was the gay district of Michigan. If so, he was going to be sorely disappointed. As far as I could tell, it was a tiny town of a few thousand inhabitants with nothing more than an elk park and a Walmart. He came back a few weeks later, and I heard nothing more of Gaylord.

Although I lost my religiosity, I kept a sense of connection to Muslims and to the Arabic language. And so, after a few months of knowing him, I asked Muhammad if he would be willing to tutor me in Arabic. One day, he came to my room. We were sitting on my bed, and I felt that he was sitting a bit too close to me. I am by nature not very confrontational, and I didn't think it was anything to complain about, so I moved a bit, making a little more space between the two of us. He moved closer, closing the gap I had created. So, I distanced myself again. And again, he moved closer. I stood up, trying to allow him to save face. I thought, *surely, you must know that you've been rebuffed. Let's just pretend that none of this ever happened, and let's continue with the Arabic lesson.*

He stood up. I acted like I was looking for something and turned my back to him. He stood right behind me, his crotch touching my butt. He was relentless. I wasn't afraid for my safety—he was tall, but I was at least as strong as he was. Still, it was the first time in my life that I felt molested. *Is this what women have to put up with?* I wondered.

I left the room, making up some reason for why I needed to leave immediately. In the months that followed, he offered several times to teach me more Arabic. I never took him up on it. I was annoyed, in truth, but I was not angry at him. Mostly, what I felt was the tragedy of the whole affair, a man attracted to men in spite of his culture, which told him that his attraction to men was sacrilegious, forced to live a double life with his loved ones and even, it seems, with himself. In the end, the only recourse he could find was to push himself on unwilling people, in an understandable yet pathetic attempt to search for companionship. He must have returned to his native Saudi Arabia by now. I wonder how he is doing sometimes. It's more than likely that he has married a woman. If so, does she know that he is attracted to men? And if she does, can she choose to leave if she wants to? Probably not. Such are the fruits of social repression.

CHAPTER 29

The Champollion of Love

From ages six to 15, I attended all-boys Catholic schools. I was also a religious puritan for whom the very idea of dating, let alone having sex, was sinful. At age 12, when I discovered the character of Frollo in *The Hunchback of Notre Dame*, I felt that I had met a kindred spirit. Like him, I had aspirations of intellectualism and religious austerity, and I was revolted at the thought that I should be subject to such detestable feelings as lust. How was it that I, in spite of all my efforts to be saintly, could be filled with desires I did not wish to have?

The result of this doomed fight against nature was that I was exceedingly awkward in front of women, torn between a desire for companionship and a wish to maintain a self-imposed image of holiness. The extent of my dating history was that for a year in high school, I had a girlfriend with whom I would exchange a kiss every now and then. And so, when college came, and I was finally interested in dating, I was at an impasse over how to proceed. The best I could do was to come up with two ideas, which I tested in turn.

The first of these was that maybe I could wow a girl at school or online into developing feelings for me with the sheer power of my prose. This was a four-step plan that was supposed to work this way:

Obtain her email address. This felt less invasive than asking for a phone number.

Write to her and see if she replies.

If she does, bombard her with love letters.

She falls in love with me! Right? Maybe?

Needless to say, this was an abysmal failure. For one thing, my prose, which I imagined to be in the style of Alexander Hamilton, was in reality barely comprehensible. It certainly wasn't going to make many people think of me as a romantic prospect. But that wasn't all. Some of the women I tried to woo lived far away, in one instance because she'd moved away after I met her, in the other instances because we'd met online while playing chess or checkers. I was so poor that even in the rare instances when someone seemed to be interested in me, I had no way of traveling to her. And so, having tried this to no avail, I was compelled to put an end to these hopeless endeavors after a few years, still as lonely as I'd been the day I started.

Wily as a coyote, I went back to the drawing board to come up with a new plan. I didn't know much about dating, but I did know quite a bit about video games, and I came up with what I imagined to be the brilliant idea of recasting the former in the image of the latter. Maybe dating was about accumulating points, here by giving a compliment, there with a gift, and every now and then by rendering some service. Then, having accumulated a certain number of points, one could redeem them for a reward—maybe a date, maybe a kiss, maybe something more. The more I thought about this strategy, the more pleased with myself I became. It seemed that I had discovered the Rosetta Stone of dating and would soon be recognized as the Champollion of love. I couldn't have known it at the time, but I was well on my way to developing a severe case of nice guy syndrome. This plan of mine, of course, didn't work any better than the previous one. In fact, it had even worse results, leaving me not only lonely but also entitled and aggrieved. *How dare these women not return my affections after I had been so very nice to them? Couldn't they see that I was a much better catch than the other guy they were interested in?* They could see no such thing, precisely because there was no such thing to see. Inexperienced and emotionally stunted, I was the very opposite of a good catch. And I was certainly no Champollion, however delusional I might be about the subject.

It was not until I was 21 that I finally met a young woman who somehow thought that I was someone worth dating. I think she was wrong about that. I was a rather terrible boyfriend, in truth, and we were incompatible in several ways. I was like a wild animal who needed a lot of training, and I will always be grateful that she was there to domesticate me. But we'll get to that later.

CHAPTER 30

A Long Night

I hate moving. It's not just that I hate taking apart and putting together furniture, and lifting boxes full of accumulated old books that I only interact with when I am relocating to a new home. Part of the problem is that I never quite realize how much stuff I own until it's time to move. Then, I make a resolution to own fewer things. I donate or throw out everything I can get rid of, only to find myself wondering during the next move how I could possibly have let myself purchase so many unnecessary things. But there are some possessions I will never part with. One of these is a short-sleeved blue shirt that is emblazoned with the logo of the Mobil Corporation. It's an old work uniform, from my first year of college, when I was an associate at a gas station. It's become a precious object, half talisman, half reminder of how far I've come and the hard times I've been through.

And there were definitely some hard times. I had constant anxiety over whether I would be permitted to stay in my adoptive country. This, combined with a deep feeling of loneliness, led me to a period of deep depression in which I would casually mention my thoughts of suicide at the first start of frustration. Two things saved me during those years. The first was that, much as I wanted to die, I did not want to suffer, and I couldn't think of a way to bring about the former without the latter. The second was that two of the people I mentioned my thoughts of suicide to referred me to a university psychologist, who helped me navigate my difficulties by challenging me to think about what I could do to change the things I didn't like about my life.

One of the things that therapy could not change, however, was my dire financial situation. The gas station was a 45-minute drive away from school. So, when an opportunity to work as a sitter just a 20-minute drive away presented itself, I jumped on it. This was at the beginning of nursing school, in 2005. My job was to stay by the side of patients who were not safe by themselves, either because they would try to stand up when they weren't supposed to, or because they would try to pull out their IV tubing or tear off their bandages. The pay was $8 an hour, which was acceptable enough.

Some shifts were so easy that I could grab a book and read for several hours, which as far as I was concerned made this the best job ever. But there were more difficult days, like the time I was watching over an agitated man with a traumatic brain injury. He was crying about the loss of his one true love and constantly repeating her name—Christie. He would throw away his urinal, point his penis straight up and shoot streams of urine all around the room. I am not ashamed to admit that in those moments, I was not brave enough to stay by his bed. I had never heard of golden showers, but it was clear to me that this was not something I wanted any part of. I scurried into the corner of the room, fervently praying that the unwelcome rain would not reach me.

The shifts in which I had to watch over confused patients trying to pull out their IVs could also be eventful. On one occasion, tired of the incessant wrestling, I decided to try a different approach. There was an old lady, probably in her 70s, who was trying to grab me. Not fearing for my safety, I decided to let her go for it, figuring that this was better than having her toy with the equipment. Eventually, after pulling on my arm and my shirt to no avail, she started standing up. I got closer in order to prevent her from falling, and at that moment realized that this was what she'd wanted all along—she was actually trying to pull me into bed with her! Suppressing my amusement—I would have been on the floor laughing if I hadn't been at work in a hospital—I managed with some effort to disentangle myself from her grip and set her back into bed, and not a moment too soon. Her husband and grandson arrived a minute later and, to my amazement, she was perfectly lucid with them. She had known exactly what she was doing!

I recall sitting with a 15-year-old boy who had suffered a traumatic brain injury and who was restless. He wasn't violent or screaming, but he just couldn't seem to lie still. He pulled at all manner of things, including me. Again, confident that nothing untoward would happen, I decided to stop resisting for a bit. Before I knew it, he was bear hugging me and landing a kiss on my temple! I immediately extricated myself from his embrace, looked around to confirm that there had been no witness, and allowed myself a hearty laugh. Maybe this was not the best way to deal with agitated patients, after all. I saw the boy months later, and he was doing well. I walked up to him, asked him if he remembered me, and told him that he had kissed me. I suppose I expected him to be as amused by the story as I had been. Instead, he was horrified, and left without saying a word. I was a smart kid, but I was not very wise.

If there is one thing that's better than $8 per hour, it's $9 per hour, which is what you could earn if you were a sitter on a night shift. I had worked night shifts before at the gas station, and found that I could stay awake as long as I had something to read. This seemed like a great deal, especially given that all my sitter colleagues who had worked night shifts assured me that you could sleep a bit. That did it! I signed up for a night shift, expecting something easy. I was going to get paid to read and sleep, two of my favorite activities. My first inkling that things weren't going to go as I had anticipated was that I was placed in the Trauma Burn Unit. The patient needed to be watched. His family had been by his side, but they needed a break. His sister was there when I arrived. She explained how he had been behaving, and it didn't seem like anything I couldn't handle. I sat by his bedside in a large, comfortable reclining chair. I had a dim light by which I could read. All was well. The nurse came to ask me if I was comfortable. I was. She handed me some blankets, which I very much appreciated. After less than an hour of reading, however, I was told that the light had to be turned off because excessive stimulation is bad for patients with brain injuries. So now, I found myself sitting in the dark, in a reclining chair, with a blanket over me. It would be hard to design a better soporific.

The first thing I noticed is that I kept waking up. *I'm awake! I'm awake,* I'd say to myself. Then, I would check on the patient, realize that he was doing well, and the next thing I knew, I was waking up again. After a few rounds of this *I'm awake* routine, I noticed that I was not alone. Peering down at me was the face of a very unhappy woman. It was the patient's sister, understandably irate at finding the watchman who had been hired to watch over her brother asleep.

"Had a long night?" she asked in a voice that barely concealed her anger.

My command of English failed me here. I wasn't quite sure what the expression meant, and her sarcasm definitely went over my head. What I should have said was…well, was there really anything good I could have said at that point? But what I should emphatically not have said was what I did say:

"Yeah!"

I said this in an almost enthusiastic voice, as though someone had suggested to me the answer to a question I had been seeking. I seemed to be saying "Exactly! I'm so glad you understand why I'd be sitting here sleeping by your brother, even though I'm being paid to watch him! Good job! This is a great answer! I'm so proud of you for having suggested it. I'm going to adopt it as my official line. Thank you!"

Minutes later, I was gone. My shift was over. I went home and wrote a journal entry about my first night shift. I thought that all things considered, things had gone rather well. The staff had been nice. The patient had done well. I had been paid and spent much of the night sleeping.

Night shifts were a pretty good gig. I'd sign up for another one! The next day, I was unceremoniously fired over the phone. It had been reported that I had been found sleeping. Was that true? "Um, well, yes, but only a little bit," I tried to mutter. I didn't have much of a defense, in truth. I cursed myself for ever taking a night shift, but it was too late. I was now out of a job, with no savings, and without much of a plan about how to proceed. There were going to be some rough times ahead.

CHAPTER 31

Desperation

The year was 2006, and I was 20 years old. My biggest expenditure was rent at $250 per month. On top of that, Alan would ask me for an extra $100 to cover utilities every three months or so. My next single largest expenditure was my cell phone bill, which was between $50 and $60. When I was working, my after-tax income had been about $600 per month, which left me with about $300 for food and gas, plus any miscellaneous expenditures that might arise. I also had a high-interest credit card, which I had acquired in one of those since-banned drives where college students were encouraged to apply in exchange for a few slices of pizza. I was not a spendthrift, and the card had proved useful, especially when my rickety old car broke down. It had also allowed me to splurge and buy books, mostly biographies of political figures from French and American history.

It wasn't just that I'd lost my job and income. There was the added problem of my work permit, which all non-permanent residents have to apply for annually if they want to work in the US. At the time, the application fee was $180. On my meager income, it was all I could do to survive, and I had not been able to save. And soon after losing my job, my permit expired. Without the $180, if I wanted to work, it had to be under the table. So, I went on Craigslist and looked for offers. The most promising gig was a job as a personal assistant to a man with muscular dystrophy. I went to the interview and was impressed with him. He was in his mid-to-late 20s and had graduated from law school, but had not found employment. He had lost the use of his arms and legs, and needed someone to help him during the day, mostly with eating and typing. This seemed like something I could do, but I was so afraid to offend that I couldn't bring myself to ask how much he was paying.

He called me the next day to say that I had the job. I was excited. Finally, I had something. I would not starve. Shyly, I asked how much he would be paying me. I received an answer I was not prepared for: $7 per hour, which he said was equivalent to $10 per hour legally. This was manifestly not the case. $7 was not much, especially given that I would have fewer hours than in my previous job. But it was the only offer I had, so I took it. I got to know everything about this man—his obsession with Star Wars, his sense of humor, his desire for the touch of a woman, his forlorn romantic interests. It was the first time that I seriously contemplated what it must be like to live with a disability. Still, much as I liked him personally, I felt very underpaid. He also often called at the last minute to say that I wouldn't be needed because he was going to an event. These were lean and hungry months for me.

Things got bad enough in this period that there was a point where I was out of food and had no money. I turned to participating in research studies at the University of Michigan. This brought me a hundred dollars here and there, but it was still not enough. One study offered $150, the equivalent of more than 20 hours of work. I barely got through reading what it entailed before I decided to sign up. But perhaps I should have read the fine print. It was an investigation of the electrical activity of the stomach, which seemed innocuous enough. I would have to undergo an endoscopy, a procedure where a tube with an attached camera would be passed into my mouth, through my esophagus, and into my stomach. I could definitely think of other things I would rather swallow, but few of them came with money. And so, I signed up. After a brief interview in which the procedure was explained, I was told that I would need to drink a solution that would help me empty out my digestive tract.

So, I went home and took a look at the gallon-sized bottle I had been handed. The label said GOLYTELY. On the evening before the appointed day, I was to fill up the bottle up to a marked line and drink the entire thing. I did as I was told, took one sip, and immediately understood why they had stressed so many times that I needed to drink the entire bottle. It was the most disgusting thing I had ever tasted. I took a large gulp, then another one, then another one, hoping to gulp my way through the entire thing. I looked at the bottle in despair. There was an impossibly large quantity of the stuff remaining.

Goddammit.

I thought of quitting, but soon remembered the $150. I couldn't quit. I needed the money. So, I kept drinking, thinking all the while that I was literally selling my body for money. About an hour after my first sip, I realized that GOLYTELY was a complete and utter lie—there was nothing remotely light about it. I needed to go, and I needed to go *now*. I spent the rest of the night rushing to the bathroom every hour or so. And my digestive tract was disrupted for days. But at least I would have enough money to eat for the next few weeks. Of course, those few weeks were soon gone, and I was back at square one.

The bulk of my earnings went towards rent and gas. And my prospects for finding a better job with an expired work permit were bleak, to say the least. My parents were poor and couldn't help. My father had found work as a dental assistant in New York, but his pay was not great, and his expenses were high. It didn't even occur to me to ask him. I expected him to lecture me about having let my work permit expire, and I wasn't even sure that he had money to give me. I also couldn't bear to ask my mom. She was having a hard enough time making ends meet and taking care of my little sister. I knew she would be sympathetic, but I was not sure she had the means to help me.

In desperation, I confided my situation to a few people. One of these was Michael, the military veteran who was my classmate. He explained my situation to his wife, and together they made me a gift of a box of canned food, which was a literal lifesaver. The other person was Master Humesky, my tae kwon do grandmaster. He had been born in Western Ukraine in the 1920s and emigrated from there to the United States in his 30s. He had been an engineer in his younger days. We had become friends, having many conversations over the months as I drove him to and from the club. He had not said much the night when I told him about the difficulty of my situation. But, not long afterwards, he surprised me with the greatest gift anyone could have given me at the time: $180 in cash. I was stunned, and the only thing that prevented me from crying was the fact that I didn't really know how to. I wanted to turn down the gift, but I immediately felt silly. I wanted to thank him, but he would not hear of it. It was nothing, he said, and I should not mention it. So I took the money, still not sure I could believe what had just happened, and a few days later applied for my work permit. I was going to survive after all.

CHAPTER 32

Unadulterated Glee

Bureaucracies are ubiquitous in organized societies. They bring a certain level of uniformity to processes, and in so doing they create order where there would otherwise be chaos. But the flip side of this is that each person facing a bureaucratic system becomes nothing more than a replaceable part. There are no customizable solutions, because every single individual will be treated exactly the same, regardless of their particular needs and circumstances. There is a certain fairness in such a process, of course, but it can also lead to unfortunate outcomes. Sometimes you're barely making ends meet when a bounced check results in a $35 fee just a day before you're able to make a deposit into your account. This is a fee you can ill afford, and you try with the energy of desperation to reach someone, anyone, at your bank who might be able to waive it just this one time. It's all in vain. You return home crestfallen, wondering how you will be able to afford your rent.

Other times, you're applying for a license for a new state, and after dealing with the unfriendly forms, the deadlines no one made clear, the irrelevant documents they want you to provide, you are informed that it will take several weeks before your application is even processed.

The impasse is only broken when you're able to reach a human being on the other side of an icy bureaucracy, someone with whom you can make a connection, someone who can understand your plight and do something to help move things along. I was in this situation in the second half of 2006. It had to do with the ever-present need to find a way to pay for school. Simply put, I had no hope of earning enough money through work, and my parents were just as poor as they had ever been. So, without expecting much, and just seeking an ear to listen to my frustrations, I talked to June. To my surprise, this amazing woman, who apparently doubled as my guardian angel, was again able to work her magic. She reached out to the higher-ups in the administration of Eastern Michigan University, and I was invited to a meeting. My case was discussed, and it was deemed that I was doing well enough academically that I would be given a mixture of grant and scholarship money to help me through the end of my senior year, with the stipulation that I had to maintain a certain GPA.

This was one of the most decisive breaks I ever got. I was not a very talented individual. I had never learned to play an instrument, and I had been at best mediocre at almost all the sports I had ever played. But if there was one thing I knew how to do, it was getting good grades. I had no trouble keeping my end of the bargain, and for the last year of college, I had enough grant money remaining that I no longer had to work. If I continued to live on $600 per month, I would have just enough money to make it through April 2007, at the end of which I would graduate. I made sure to line up a job, which I started exactly seven days after graduation. I had run out of money by then, but Josh was kind enough to lend me $1,000, which I repaid over a few months. My financial troubles were finally behind me. There was much here to celebrate, but there was more good news still to come.

In December 2006, my family returned before a judge for yet another immigration hearing. My father was silent. But my mom and I were chatted up by a friendly African American man who kept cracking jokes. To our surprise, when we entered the courtroom, the irrepressible jokester was actually the government counsel! He was our adversary! This was unexpected for us because at every one of our previous hearings, it had been a woman dressed in what seemed like the most expensive designer clothes in the universe. She also had the most unfriendly demeanor I had ever encountered. I could never in a million years have imagined her trading greetings with us, let alone jokes. Perhaps this was a good sign?

We waited expectantly. As the judge was reading her opinion, I could feel the timbre of her voice change as she was reaching the climax of the decision. I looked at my father and gave a thumbs up, taking the precaution to hide my movements behind the bench. He frowned, growled, and quickly motioned for me to stop, as though he were afraid that I would jinx it all at this late juncture. I complied. I was confident we had it in the bag, so I didn't mind being reprimanded. It was only a matter of time now. I was right. Before long, the judge reached the end of her decision. It was over. We really had been granted asylum. I could scarcely believe it. Never before and never since have I been as elated, as exhilarated, as filled with sheer unadulterated glee, as I was in that moment. It was only then, in that instant of supreme serenity, as my cares were lifted from my shoulders, that I realized just how much anguish, how much fear, and how much stress years of living as a semi-undocumented immigrant had put me under. I was free at last. For the first time since arriving in the country five years earlier, I no longer feared for my future. For the first time, I could have certainty that my academic work would not be in vain. For the first time, America had truly accepted me as one of its own. I really had won the life lottery.

CHAPTER 33

Some Counterihtuitive Aspećts of Immigration Policy

This story of mine is unique, as every story describing the life of an individual is. Yet it's impossible for me to think of my story without considering the wider notion of immigration. Every sovereign nation, of course, retains the right to regulate who will be admitted and accepted as a naturalized citizen. And if laws are to be respected, there need to be consequences for those who break them. But in our rush to be punitive, we sometimes design policies that are detrimental the nation as a whole. Recently, a rule was adopted in the US to disqualify any immigrant who has used public assistance from the path to permanent residency. The rationale here is easy enough to discern. The idea is that the country should focus on taking in educated people who can fully support themselves. In this context, people like my mother—an immigrant with two children and without a college degree—should not be welcome, given that they are more likely than others to use more in public assistance than they bring in through taxes. Granting permanent status to such immigrants would only encourage the immigration of more like them to this country. The argument, then, is that insofar as the country spends more on these people than it gets in tax revenue, it is a net loss to grant them legal status.

The problem with this line of reasoning is that its analysis of the impact of immigrants with low education levels is simplistic and incorrect. Counterintuitive though it may be, even poor immigrants who use public assistance have a positive effect on the federal budget. It is true that at the state and local levels, immigrants with low education achievements initially have a negative impact on the budget, given that they generally have larger families and make greater use of public resources such as school for their children. But in the long run, this is more than compensated for by the upward mobility of these children, who end up paying much more in taxes than they ever used in benefits. The benefits of immigration make sense if you think about the history of the US. For the most part, it wasn't rich, educated Europeans who left their various countries to settle in the US. It was the poor, as it has always been. People who are doing well in their own country, where they can speak their own language and interact with their lifelong friends and family on a daily basis, don't tend to leave. It is the hungry and disaffected who set out in search of a better life. One classic example of this is the Irish people who left their homeland during the Great Famine. Then, as now, the new immigrants were met with nativism and predictions that they were too foreign to successfully assimilate. And yet, after a few generations, their descendants became American enough to become nativist themselves. And few will argue that taking in those poor immigrants was a net cost to the country. Poor as they were, their children and grandchildren became as industrious as the rest of the population and contributed to the wealth of the nation. That's how it's always been.

I suspect that the opposition to granting permanent residency and citizenship to immigrants is not grounded in economics or in fiscal concerns. Rather, it is grounded in nativism and cultural animosity. It would be unfortunate if we allowed such feelings to dictate the form of our immigration policy. Consider that there was a time, a mere 13 years ago, when I didn't have enough money to eat. I could have used some help. I was a college student in nursing school, and I was certainly not going to abandon my studies on account of receiving some food stamps. I was soon to graduate and start supporting myself. I just needed some temporary assistance. Now, suppose that I had used some public assistance and that the new proposed policy had been in effect. I would have been denied permanent residency. Without being a legal resident, I would have been ineligible to gain admission to med school. Consider that as a physician, in my first full year of work alone, I paid more in taxes than I used to make in an entire year as a nurse. This amount dwarfs anything I would have received in the form of food stamps. It will come as no surprise that I do not feel that such punitive proposals help the country in the long run.

CHAPTER 34

A Very Good Boy

She was 22 and I was 21. It was my last semester of nursing school. She had two more years to go. She was a petite brunette, a whole foot shorter than me, with piercing light-blue eyes. We met in the library. She had approached me on some excuse. She was flirting. I can now see that, but I didn't know it at the time. Besides, she was too pretty. And pretty girls like that usually weren't interested in me. Still, when it was time to part ways on that first day, it seemed that she wanted to talk again. Giving her my phone number or asking for hers seemed too presumptuous. Or maybe I was just clueless. In any case, all I could think to do was exchange emails. Somehow, she wasn't turned off by the clues I kept missing. She wrote and mentioned that she had noticed me a few weeks before and had been wanting to talk to me since then. She confessed that she was afraid this might scare me off. I did what I did best, writing back in my usual almost-professorial tone. My message included passages such as this:

"…when I graduated from high school, I had never even given thought to the idea of becoming a nurse. But circumstances often lead us to paths we never envisaged we would tread on. In this case, although I must say my intellect has

come to approve of the choice life made for me, my heart has still not been won ... and never truly will, I fear."

"Why do you write like that?" A woman who was no longer speaking to me had asked me this the year before. I had taken it to mean that her reading comprehension was deficient, or that she was simply not intellectual enough for me. It hadn't occurred to me that she might have wanted to talk to someone who sounded more like a human than a book. But I was lucky with Ashley—she decided to write back. It was a good thing, too, because I had finally picked up on her hints and had found the courage to finish my professorial email with, "When will you next be on campus? We could get together for lunch or something and I could learn more about you. Oh, by the way, you shouldn't worry about scaring me. Your smile is much too beautiful for that."

Soon enough, we were dating. I liked her company. I liked her small hands. I liked her tiny nose. I liked her blue eyes. I liked above all that I had found someone who liked me. But there was a problem. The last time I had dated anyone was in high school, four years before. And apart from some cuddles and pecks on the mouth that I mistook to be romantic kisses, I hadn't been physical with my high school girlfriend. So, when Ashley tried to kiss me, it very soon became apparent that I had no idea what to do with my tongue. The mechanics of where and how to move your tongue, and how much pressure to apply, were not anything I had read about in a book. And now, my inexperience showed.

But that was far from the worst of it. I had been in embarrassing situations where I had tried to console a female friend who was crying with a hug, when suddenly, out of nowhere, I could feel a bulge in my pants that I knew my friend must be feeling too. This was followed first by the horrifying thought that she might think I was somehow turned on by her crying, and second by an awkward side hug in a hopeless attempt to hide what was already much too late to hide. I had the following dialogue playing inside my head all the while:

"Huh, Dick? What are you doing?"

"Come on! There's a woman in your arms. Party time! Am I right?"

"No, Dick. This is, like, really, really not the time."

Sometimes, your dick is just going to be a dick.

With Ashley, I had the opposite problem. This phallic companion of mine, who had so often proudly shown himself where he hadn't been invited, was all of a sudden unwilling to show up, deserting me in my hour of need now that the so-longed-for party was at hand. I was nervous, very nervous, and very anxious to hide this from her. The result was that every time she touched me anywhere below my navel, the tumescent organ that had only moments before seemed so eager to defy gravity would shrink, shrivel out of sight, and stubbornly refuse to respond to any attempt at resuscitation. Sometimes, your dick is just going to be a dick.

Then I would have to spend the rest of what was supposed to have been sexy time trying to reassure her that I was actually very much attracted to her, even as I was secretly dealing with my own internal fear that some curse had been placed on me that would forever prevent me from having sex. She would leave, and my dear friend down there in my pants—this traitor, this Judas, this backstabber who steadfastly refused to stab frontwards—would immediately resume his ascent to his previous position. I would exclaim in disgust and indignation, "Where the hell were YOU when I needed you earlier?" But of course, sometimes your dick is just going to be a dick.

At last, after a few weeks during which the trial and error gradually morphed into trial and success, Ashley asked me a question she'd been meaning to ask:

"Habib, are you a good boy?"

"I don't know what you're talking about."

"Are you, like, a *really* good boy?"

I knew exactly what she meant. I had been a good boy. I had been a *very* good boy. But thanks to her, at age 21, I was no longer so good.

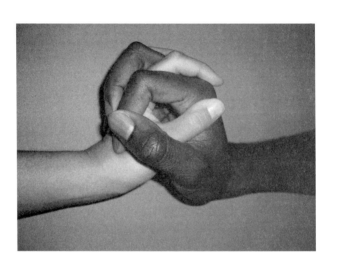

CHAPTER 35

Holding Hands

It's 2007.

We're on campus.

I'm Black.

She's White.

We're holding hands.

A man is sitting in his car,

An air of intensity etched into his face.

He's looking at something.

He's looking at *us!*

I'm curious.

Looks like he wants to say something.

We're walking towards him.

We'll get there soon enough.

We get close.

He sticks out his head.

Maybe he's lost.

Maybe he needs directions.

I give him a friendly glance.

"This is the most disgusting thing in the world. Completely makes me sick," he says.

He spits at us and quickly drives off.

We're too stunned to respond.

By the time we can move or speak, he's long gone.

The intense look on his face comes back to haunt my thoughts.

That look … that was the face of hatred.

CHAPTER 36

Email Exchanges

- -

From: Habib Fanny
Sent: Sun 3/11/2007 7:43 PM
To: CONSIGLIO, DAVID A

Bonjour Monsieur,

I have good news. I just saved a bunch of money on my car insurance by switching to Geico!

No, on a more serious note, I had an interview today for a registered nurse position at the U of M hospital, at the end of which I was told, "Welcome to the University of Michigan," which I understood to be a job offer. I am to start in early May, about a week after graduation. What is great is that I will have the opportunity to work three 12-hour shifts every week. What makes it all the more valuable is that, having no family life at the moment, I truly don't mind working every weekend. If I work Friday through Sunday every week, not only will I get pay bonuses at the end of the month, but I will be able to take classes while I work full time. I have 8 more pre-med classes to take. I should be able to complete them within a year if I keep such a schedule! Apparently, life is like everyone else: when she's tired of frowning at you, she smiles. She has such a wonderful smile...I wonder why she doesn't smile more often.

Habib

From: "CONSIGLIO, DAVID A"
To: Habib Fanny
Sent: Mon 3/12/2007, 6:18 AM

Hello!

What truly superlative news, although I am certainly not surprised to hear of your continuing success. There are few students I know who would view the scheduling of work on the weekends and class on weekdays as a positive development, but that only shines the light of truth on their unwillingness to work hard to achieve their dreams. Following the completion of 2 semesters of pre-med coursework, where will you stand academically? Will you then apply to med schools or will you have additional undergraduate work to complete?

As always, I wish you more smiles than frowns. My alma mater has just become a better school with your addition. This, of course, reflects positively on me, and as such I approve.

David Consiglio, Jr.
Southfield-Lathrup High School
AP Chemistry / Chemistry / Physics Teacher

From: Habib Fanny
Sent: Mon 3/12/2007 11:33 AM
To: CONSIGLIO, DAVID A

I merely see myself as very fortunate. The 8 classes I mentioned are all that remains to be taken before I can apply to medical school. Two semesters is an optimistic figure. Those classes will not be easy ones. It is possible that in light of the weight of their courseload I may have to take them over a period longer than a year. But it doesn't hurt to try to take them all in two semesters. If I can succeed while I am working 36 hours every week, it will probably be the greatest achievement of my life. But in truth does it really matter whether I complete those classes in a year or two? No, in the greater scheme of things, apart from perhaps the fact that I will have one more year of salary, it matters not. But, if I do, I will obtain my medical degree at age 26, [the] age at which my father obtained his doctorate in dental surgery. It's that simple, it's that dumb, but I can't get myself to abandon the desire to do as well as my father, even though I know that the system in which he studied was different and that there are actually two grade levels that he had to do over.

As always, though, I plan, but I am conscious of the fact that circumstances may decide otherwise. I don't know if you recall it, but four years ago, I proclaimed to anyone who would hear it that if there was one thing I was sure I did not want to study, it was medicine. Nursing was not anything I would have even considered. But life has decided otherwise. But if the past is to be a guide, I have no reason to fear: "everything's gonna be all right."

Habib

CHAPTER 37

Fly to the Moon

Today, as a physician, I am kind to new nurses. I remember the days right after graduating from nursing school. Physicians who finish med school get several years of training under supervision. It was altogether different in the nursing field when I started work in 2007. In those days, you would get about a month of supervision, and you were subtly encouraged to get through this period of tutelage as fast as you could. It was hard work, and it required a lot of organization and discipline. I made mistakes, again, and again, and again. I absolutely hated it. Since my income had quadrupled, and since I was concurrently enrolled in pre-med classes, I decided that I would work as little as I could get away with. Whenever we were overstaffed, I'd volunteer to go home early. I didn't want to be there. The problem was that people started thinking that I was lazy, and my every mistake was interpreted through the prism of my perceived indolence.

I had colleagues who watched me and reported every one of my mistakes to the nurse manager, who soon concluded that she had made a mistake in hiring me. There was also some hazing behavior, like the time I forgot to write the date on a feeding tube bag I had started. Instead of pulling me aside to give me some advice, one nurse decided that the best thing she could do was remove the dirty, used bag from the patient's room, affix to it a Post-it Note with her complaint, and set it in my mailbox. Once, I was accused of diverting some benzodiazepines. It was a ridiculous charge. I didn't drink alcohol—I wouldn't have my first drink until age 25—and I had never smoked a cigarette. I was so against the idea of using mind-altering substances that I didn't even drink coffee. But the manager had such a low opinion of me that she was ready to believe the accusation. I was sent home early from my shift. A few hours later, I was exonerated after the medication-dispensing machine was checked. I did not receive an apology.

I am fairly certain that if I hadn't found another job, I would have been fired. The manager must have been relieved to see me go. I thought that she would tell my new manager all kinds of negative things about me, but she did no such thing. And so, having worked for a year and a half on my first unit, I left the pulmonary floor and started working in psychiatry, which was much gentler. In fact, as a night-shift nurse, my main responsibility was to ensure that my patients got some rest. This was a much more congenial atmosphere, and it allowed me to have a relatively low-stress job as I worked on finishing my pre-med coursework.

Sometimes, the night shift was so placid that I wondered why I was getting paid. But there were also some nights that I will remember for as long as I live. One time we found an old woman unresponsive, probably already dead in her bed, but with her body warm enough to convince us to attempt to revive her. We called a code, people came rushing in, and pretty soon, we were furiously performing chest compressions. After 10 minutes of CPR, the resident on call decided to call it quits and asked if anyone had an objection. I wanted to step forward and raise my hand. I felt that she had not just died, but that I personally had failed to save her. Although I felt guilty, I saw that no one around me thought that there was any use continuing with the attempt to revive her, so I resigned myself and went home. It was months before I was able to discuss this event with anyone.

But the psych ward was not always such a dark place to work. Being a charge nurse at night wasn't always enjoyable—some staff members consistently showed up late, and, when they were not sleeping on the job, seemed intent to do as little work as humanly possible. I also had to call security to restrain and medicate a belligerent patient every now and then. But for the most part, the work was pleasant. It was also on the psych ward that I met Alex, the man who became my closest friend. He was a patient care worker (PCW), the cumbersome and grandiloquent title we used for nurse's aides on the unit. He was three years younger than me, more than half a foot shorter, and possessed of a stocky build and an aquiline nose. We bonded over our shared frustration with the indolence of some of the staff, and we soon developed a friendship that revolved around playing tennis, watching *House,* and discussing our hopes and future plans. Like me, he dreamed of going to med school someday. During our first interaction, he asked me if I could help him change a patient who had soiled herself.

"Can't you ask the other PCW?"

"Yeah, but…"

"But?"

"It's Brandon."

"Oh…"

There was nothing else to add. Brandon was a man in his mid-to-late 30s who'd only gotten the job because his father was a psychiatrist in the department. He was utterly lacking in interpersonal skills and completely incapable of properly discharging his duties. It took longer to finish tasks with his help than without it. I got up to help Alex. We cleaned the patient and changed her diaper. He thanked me for helping, when so many other nurses on the unit would have blown him off.

"No worries, man. I know why you asked me to help. He's like negative help!"

"Negative Help! That's what we should call him from now on."

We laughed. It was not the last time we would give someone an irreverent nickname. But there was more to being on the psych ward than making friends and giving people creative nicknames. I also needed to decide what kind of nurse I was going to be. At first, I was very reticent to give agitated patients intramuscular injections against their will. I had a philosophy that it was better to obtain a person's cooperation without pharmaceuticals, and I adhered to it as much as I could. Part of it came from witnessing a pattern of behavior by some nurses that sickened me. They would be rude to a patient or abuse their power by revoking privileges without due cause. Some patients would respond in anger, and some nurses, instead of trying to diffuse the tension, would see it as a challenge and respond in an authoritarian manner almost calculated to provoke more anger. Then, with the patient suitably agitated, they would call security and forcibly administer an injection of an antipsychotic.

I witnessed this so many times—many from one particularly abrasive nurse, who would end up getting fired—that I decided to define myself as the antithesis of such behavior. But in retrospect, I took things too far. There were some instances where I could have saved myself and the patient a lot of distress if I had moved to administer some medication a bit faster. One such instance happened with a woman in her mid-to-late 40s. All night long, Alex kept asking if I thought it would be a good idea to medicate her. Each time, I refused, thinking that she would calm down of her own accord. She just needed to be redirected and everything would be fine. It was very easy for me to cling to my theory of the superiority of non-pharmaceutical interventions, especially given that I was not the one watching over her.

Around 5 AM, her agitation worsened, and I could no longer ignore it. I tried to calm her down, believing that somehow my words would succeed where others had failed before. The first inkling I got that this wasn't going to work was when she threatened to dump the urine we had been collecting in her bathroom on me. I hastily retreated to confer with my staff outside her room. When I reentered, I thought I would sit down in order to be as unthreatening as I could. So, I grabbed a chair, turned it backwards and sat astride it, with my arms folded. I thought things were going well until she said, "I'm gonna hit youuuu," as she waved her fist in my face.

I was 23 years old, about twice her size, and with a black belt in tae kwon do. I was skeptical of the danger of her threat. *You're not going to hit me any more than I'm going to grow wings right now and fly to the moon!* I didn't actually say this, but she could decipher my thoughts from the smirk on my face, which was basically prodding her to go ahead and make my day. And so, she did, sending her fist towards the left side of my face, and leaving me only enough time to turn my head to avoid being hit in the eye. We froze for a second, and then I slowly opened the eyes I had shut during the impact. I was unharmed, but stunned that she had actually hit me. As I pondered my next move, the stillness was broken.

"You're not gonna cry now, are you?" She was mocking me!

"Are you happy now?" I asked, half exasperated, half amused.

"Yes," she said, matter-of-factly.

"Good. Now you're going in restraints."

But when I returned to her room with the restraints, she was perfectly calm. The restraints were no longer necessary, and I wasn't going to apply them merely as punishment. I shrugged as I left her room. I guess she must have just needed to punch someone in the face.

CHAPTER 38

Eunuch

When I met Matt, he was in his mid-20s. I was a nurse working on the psych floor at the University of Michigan Hospital. He was a patient care technician. Tall, dark-haired, and clever as a devil, he had an immense talent for getting under your skin with surgical precision. He was a fun guy to be around, and occasionally, we would hang out outside of work.

One day, we were having a discussion about religion, and I had given my standard line: I had grown up religious, but I had now decided that I was no fan of organized religion. So now, I was an agnostic. Without missing a beat, he replied, "You know an agnostic is just an atheist without balls, right?"

I hated hearing that. I thought it was an asinine and puerile comment. I defended myself with all the fury I could muster. I was the reasonable one. Atheism was a faith. I wasn't cowardly. And I sure as hell wasn't a damn eunuch. It was just that I found my position the most logically defensible, in light of the fact that there was no evidence of the existence of God either way. Why couldn't people see that? He wasn't even bothering to counter my arguments, but I was on a roll, and I couldn't stop arguing. And the whole time he stood there smirking at me. He had pushed me where I was tender, and he knew it. I knew it, too. And because I knew it, it was not at him that my words were aimed; it was at myself.

We changed the subject and then I went home determined to put this whole idiotic affair behind me. *An atheist without balls! Screw him.* I wasn't emasculated by my fear of offending people. I resolved to think no more of it. But I could no more will myself to stop thinking of it than a jilted lover can will himself into forgetting the object of his unrequited love. The thoughts stayed with me. *Atheist without balls. Emasculated. Eunuch. Castrated. Coward.* For months afterwards—long after he had forgotten that he had pushed my buttons—I was still obsessing over these words. It had nothing to do with him. I was wrestling with myself. *Was I an agnostic because I was afraid to admit that I didn't believe?* That couldn't be. I repeated my logical reasons for eschewing atheism. They rang hollow.

Then, one day, someone brought up God and I surprised myself with the vehemence with which I rejected the idea. Before this, I hadn't said anything out loud, but now it was impossible to deny it: I didn't believe in God, not even a little. Did that make me...? I couldn't bear to even think of the word. I tried to avoid saying such a sacrilegious thing. I felt that a certain spell would be broken, that I would reach a point of no return if I dared to call myself an atheist. And yet, there it was. I had thought it in spite of myself. The word scared me. It was as though I had picked up a hot object and was reflexively trying to drop it. But the object stuck to my hand. This was a burn I could not avoid. I thought of God. I wanted to ask him to forgive me for committing the great sin of not believing in him. *God, please…* I couldn't pray. I felt silly. I laughed at myself. Was there really no God? Were we really all alone, without protection in an uncaring universe? I didn't want to believe that, but it rang truer than the alternative. I was an atheist. I had been an atheist for a while, I realized. How long? A year? Two years? Three years? I did not know.

Then I realized that I would die someday, and that I would truly die and cease to exist. Again, I was afraid. I didn't want to stop existing. I imagined non-existence as a cold, dark place where I was sentient but deprived of all my senses. I imagined spending an eternity unable to communicate with anyone, bemoaning the fact that I no longer existed. It took me several more months to realize that non-existence meant that I would be too dead to understand that I was dead. I thought of the people I had known who had died. I had told myself that I would see them again, someday. Now I believed that they were truly dead. I thought of my parents, who were in their 50s. In two or three decades, they too would be dead. All of a sudden, I understood why so many people fiercely believed. I didn't want to die and I didn't want to lose my parents forever. Again, I tried to talk to God. He said nothing back. There was no God. There was just me, and my fears, and my hopes, and my dreams, and this fragile and finite life of mine that was slowly running out.

CHAPTER 39

The Rational Thing

During my years as a nurse, school was both my biggest challenge and my number-one priority. I had taken Uncle Mory's advice to go to med school, and by now, I had thoroughly warmed to the idea. In my initial optimism, I had sounded like my mom: I was going to work full time and go to school full time, and I was going to get amazing grades, and I was going to finish all my pre-reqs in one year, and I was going to start med school immediately afterwards, and I was going to graduate after four years—at or near the top of my class—and I was going to enter a super-competitive field, because I was Superman and I could do it all. But life had other plans for me.

The first thing I learned was that I wasn't going to be able to work three 12-hour shifts, as I had anticipated. Instead, it was two 12-hour shifts and two eight-hour ones, making a total of 40 hours each week. I was going to have to be judicious about when I could work and how many classes I could take at a time. I decided that my two 12-hour shifts would be every weekend, and this was easily accepted since other nurses preferred to have their weekends off with their families. This meant that my two eight-hour shifts would be on weekdays, leaving me with plenty of time to take classes. But I soon discovered that I had a limit. If I wanted an A in all of my classes, the most I could do was two four-credit courses per semester. Working less wasn't an option—I was paying for my classes out of pocket, so if I reduced my hours to make time for more classes, I wouldn't be able to pay for school.

Slowly I worked my way through my classes. The most challenging were the two semesters of organic chemistry I had to take. I had never had to study much before. Getting an A had always been a matter of glancing at my notes and solving problems a few hours before my tests. But I remember having a moment of panic in organic chemistry when I realized a week before a test that I would fail if I were to take the exam right then and there. I ended up getting an A, but I had needed to start studying two full days before the exam, which seemed like an excessive amount of time. In Ivory Coast, what we students had admired most were not people who got good grades after spending a lot of time studying—which we thought anyone could do—but those who could get good grades with minimal effort. I had, it seems, internalized this conception of what it meant to be intelligent, and in the process failed to develop good study habits. But for the time being, it didn't matter. I didn't realize it at the time, but the volume of information to be learned was still low enough that study habits were of little pertinence.

And so, without too much difficulty I completed my pre-med classes over two years. Then I started studying for the MCAT over the course of a month. My preparation was doing the minimal amount of reading, a fair number of practice questions, and listening to MCAT Audio Osmosis while playing video games. I had been a good student, and I had a high fund of knowledge at baseline, so this study regimen that would have been highly inadequate for most people ended up being enough for me. My score placed me in the 87th percentile of test takers.

"Dude, you're about to be a doctor!" Alex said.

"I don't know about that, man. I haven't even applied yet."

"Dude! You're about to be a doctor."

I continued to downplay it. It wasn't that I didn't realize how good my chances were to get into med school—my result wasn't spectacular, but it was definitely enough to get into med school. But the road ahead was very long indeed: another year before I would start med school, then four years of school, then another four or five years of residency training. Celebration at this point seemed very premature.

"Dude, you're about to be a doctor," Alex kept repeating.

"How about let me get in first?"

"But dude..."

"What?"

"You're about to be a doctor!"

He was decidedly more excited than me. For the time being, all I could think of was completing the cumbersome application process. I sent applications to about 15 schools. After several interview offers, I was accepted at five of them. Of these, the University of Iowa was not only the highest-ranked school, but also the one that offered enough scholarship assistance to cover my tuition. It was a very easy decision.

Grateful as I was for the acceptance and scholarship, I couldn't help but reflect on the nature of affirmative action. I have no doubt that I would have been admitted to a medical school without affirmative action, given that I applied with a 3.7 science GPA and a 32 on the MCAT. But would I have gotten as many acceptances? It's doubtful, and it's even less likely that I would have been offered tuition-free med school. I knew many White and Asian students with better grades than me who had borrowed money to pay for their medical education. Many of these people started life with more advantages than I did, but some graduated with $200,000 more student loan debt than I did. I was very conscious of the fact that my ancestors had not been enslaved, and had not suffered under Jim Crow. True, I had been poor after moving to the US— poor enough that a mere two years before applying to med school, I had gone hungry. But did that have anything to do with my race? My family was poor primarily for two reasons: my father had not saved and invested enough during his two decades as a dentist in Ivory Coast, and we were African immigrants. What counts as wealth in a West African context—where there are millions of people living in abject poverty, and where labor is consequently cheap—is not worth much in an American context. I wondered whether affirmative action was really the best way to help impoverished African Americans. The system favors Black immigrants from educated families and middle- and upper-middle-class African Americans. Poor people of any race are more in need of assistance than these groups. Wouldn't it be fairer and more politically sustainable to base scholarship assistance on socioeconomic status, irrespective of race?

But however ambivalent I was, I was fully conscious of two inescapable facts. First, I did not have $200,000 to pay for my education, and refusing money I was freely offered would be foolish. Second, if I were to refuse the money, it would do nothing to change the system, and the money would find its way to someone else. The scholarship I received was from private donors who strongly believed in increasing diversity at the University of Iowa, one of the Whitest states in the country. They had simply put their money where their mouth was, so to speak. And so, I did the rational thing and took the money, resolving to pay it forward someday when I got the chance.

CHAPTER 40

Tuition

I used to look down on people with addictions. Where I was raised, addiction was seen as a character defect, not as an ailment. Steeped in that worldview, I looked down on alcoholics, and my opinion of people who used illegal substances was even lower. I remember seeing my father coming home from a night out when I was 15 years old. A taxi dropped him off outside our home. He was drunk, reeked of alcohol, and could barely stand up. Filled with disappointment and disgust, I watched him titubate his way towards the door. To my austere Muslim eyes, there could be no sight worse than a father drunk in front of his own child. A few minutes later, I was told that he was calling me. I felt that I had seen quite enough of him that night, but I didn't know how to disobey a direct command, so I hid my emotions and went. I found him utterly unable to remember that he had asked for me. The next day, he was back to normal and seemed to have no recollection of the previous night's events. But I couldn't forget what I had seen.

Years later, I would find myself facing my own struggles. Not with a mind-altering substance—I was still much too puritanical for such a thing—but with a habit that could have become just as destructive. It had started innocently enough, from a desire to do well financially. It occurred to me that I could save a good chunk of my income, since I was earning much more than my living expenses. But, at some point in 2007, I decided that investing was even better than saving. So, I read up on the topic and opened a brokerage account shortly afterwards. It was a bull market, and I found myself making money almost effortlessly. I had read that 90% of stock market investors lost money. I was making money, and it was very appealing to conclude from this that I must be a stock market genius. I already foresaw myself awash in cash, making millions of dollars and retiring in 10 years. Life had frowned on me for too long. Maybe this was my reward?

But it didn't last. Soon enough, the stock market took a plunge, and I was losing money—lots of it. I made the mistake of playing with money I would need the next week. And so, when my holdings went down, I was forced to quickly sell to avoid losing more money. I assumed that my losses were temporary. After all, I was a genius, and the hero of my own story. And what kind of story was this if the protagonist was just going to go down ignominiously, defeated by the stock market? It could not be. I could not let it be. And so, day after day, week after week, I continued to throw good money after bad. I justified this by convincing myself that I was just doing it to lower my overall purchase price. Sooner or later, the stocks I'd bought had to come back to their previous highs. It was just a matter of time, right?

I didn't want to admit that I had initially been the lucky beneficiary of a bull market. Whenever I wasn't working, I spent all my mornings staring at a computer screen, attempting to catch an opportunity to buy low and sell high. It never came. I was buying high and selling low. I was also addicted to day trading. There was something exhilarating about it, my rational justifications notwithstanding. But eventually, I had to admit that my theory was wrong—I was not a stock market genius. In fact, I was a damned fool. By the time I finally pulled my head out of my rear end and could see clearly again, I had lost $20,000 to $30,000 over the course of a few years. I decided to see this as tuition and promised myself that I was through with investing.

I took four years off, but in my senior year of med school, I was tempted to try again. My roommate was making a killing by investing in pot-related penny stocks. Some days he would make $1,000 to $2,000. I decided that if he could do it, so could I. So I did the stupidest thing I have ever done: I decided to borrow an extra $20,000 to invest, telling myself that at worst, my student loan debt would have increased by $20,000, and that at best, I would earn enough to repay the whole thing. It was a gamble in every sense of the term. At first, I stuck to a strategy that had worked for me in the past: I would focus on buying long-term call options on companies about to undergo a spin-off, the idea being that the sum of the parts after the spin-off would be greater than the whole had been beforehand. It was, in effect, a bet that the market was systematically underpricing companies comprising various businesses. It was possible to make money this way, but it was slow. And my roommate was making lots of money *now!* Slowly, I shifted my holdings to marijuana-related penny stocks. And immediately, I started losing money. I fell into a pattern of making riskier and riskier bets in a vain attempt to recoup all my losses in one fell swoop. After losing about $10,000, I called it quits.

I came away from this experience having learned two lessons. The first was that people who develop dependencies on substances are every bit as human as I was. They are people with addictions rather than addicts. I had not been addicted to a chemical substance, but in many ways, I had displayed much the same destructive behavior. The second was that I had run the day-trading experiment twice and learned that I was not a stock market genius. I was going to have to build wealth the slow and hard way.

CHAPTER 41

Germs on Our Side

I was a quiet child. I was a shy child. I was a pensive child. I was an odd child. I was also, it turns out, an intelligent child. For the first semester of middle school, my sister Fatou made me sit down and study before each test. And I discovered, much to my surprise, that I could get good grades with minimal effort. I didn't like studying, but I liked the sense of pride I derived from doing well academically. So, long after she stopped working with me, I continued to get good grades. In fact, this became a core part of my identity.

I disliked parties so much that several times, I unsuccessfully tried to talk my parents into just giving me money rather than throwing a birthday party. *Look, Mom, why not just give me half of what you'd spend on this party and we'll both come out ahead? You get to spend less and I don't have to clean up afterwards?* Most kids were not like me. They knew all the lyrics to the cool songs, loved partying, and would at some point experiment with drugs or alcohol or sex. To me, they seemed more interested in fitting in with their group of friends than they were in planning out their future. I fancied myself an intellectual. True, I was peculiar in many respects, but I concluded that this must be because I was a member of a natural aristocracy of intelligence, more given to intellectual pursuits than to vapid concerns such as sports, music, and parties. This is the explanation I came up with as an adolescent. Since it was more flattering to me than recognizing that I was just an odd duck who happened to be academically gifted, I believed it through high school and college. If I hadn't gone to med school, I would never have had occasion to question it.

Med school exposed me to possibilities I hadn't considered—that it was possible to be both a party animal *and* very intelligent, that a person could lift weights *and* be more than an intellectual lightweight, that you could be good at science *and* a person who'd experimented with drugs, that one could be into sports and popular culture *and* be an intellectual. In retrospect, 24 seems like a rather late age to come to such realizations, especially for someone who had prided himself on his intelligence. But it was a viewpoint based on a common fallacy—I had been seeing a cause-and-effect pattern where a mere association had existed, and this was reinforced by the fact that I wanted to see such a pattern.

Due to the intersection of culture and resource availability and the aleatory vicissitudes of history, at any given time some human civilizations will enjoy advantages over others—greater wealth, technology, military might, etc. It often happens that the people of these various civilizations have different physical attributes from one another, such as complexion, hair morphology, or height. It's tempting and more flattering to assume that any advantages derive from the intrinsically superior value of your own tribe or nation or race, rather than to random processes that would have had different outcomes if weather patterns, biodiversity, technological discoveries, and the invention and dissemination of writing had played out differently. In other words, it's easier to think, "we defeated the Native Americans because we were White, and Anglo-Saxon, and Protestant" than it is to think "we were just lucky people who happened to have germs on our side."

For some people, it's easier to think that Black people are more likely to go to jail because they are lazy, criminally minded humans of a lower order than it is to recognize that there's an inequitable distribution of wealth and opportunity coupled with more intense policing of Black people in America. In the case of my misconceptions, it was easy for me to encounter evidence that I was mistaken—there were plenty of intellectuals who didn't share my oddities and, sooner or later, I was bound to come into contact with lots of them. Socioeconomic status and the effects of imperialism tend to be sticky, however. The grandchildren of poor people are more likely to be poor than those of rich people. A formerly colonized nation is likely to be poorer than its colonizer generations after it achieves independence.

People who want to believe that they are intrinsically superior to others will never lack for data to prove to their own satisfaction that they are right. They will point to IQ tests or academic achievement gaps or higher crime rates or any manner of things that are the consequences of socioeconomic and cultural inequality. But we would do well to keep in mind that when measuring a non-dominant group in a society shaped by a dominant group using metrics developed by and for that dominant group, what we are measuring is not intelligence or intrinsic worth but cultural assimilation or possession of traits valued by the dominant culture. Racism, in the end, is nothing more than the inability and unwillingness to extend to the other, however defined, the benefit of the doubt and the presumption of common humanity.

CHAPTER 42

Jesus

There are some people who enjoy the med school experience. They thrive. They collect accolade after accolade. They proudly present the fruits of their research endeavors at national conferences. They get stratospheric scores on board exams. Their letters of recommendation are glowing. Everyone talks about their achievements in superlative terms. Because school had always been easy, in my undergrad years I had expected that this would be my experience in med school as well. The expectation was confirmed when I got a perfect score on the first test of the year, in biochemistry. I was in heaven. I imagined the rest of med school going much as that test had gone, although I humbly acknowledged that I would miss a question every now and then.

But within a semester of starting med school, I found myself thinking *this was a mistake* and *I hate my life*. The first two years of med school are about acquiring the scientific foundation required to understand how the structure and function of the body can go awry. During these years, if you want to do well, you need to treat attending classes and studying as a full-time job. At my school, every week there was a big test that covered roughly the same amount of material as an undergrad midterm exam. And truth be told, I didn't like the subjects I was studying. Chemistry and physics had always come naturally to me. Biology? Not so much. You couldn't derive things from first principles. As best I could tell, it was a bunch of memorization and regurgitation. I knew medicine was founded on biology more than anything else, but I had convinced myself that since I was smart, I could learn anything, my personal emotions be damned.

It was I who was damned. Damned to years of misery and depression, damned to dreaming that maybe next year would be better, only to realize that, no, it didn't really get better after all. For the first time in my life, I struggled. It was hard for me to focus on my studies, and hard to absorb all the material I was supposed to learn. My girlfriend at the time, who was one of the best students of medicine I have ever encountered, thought I had undiagnosed ADHD. It was a fine theory, but the idea of taking stimulants felt like cheating, so I didn't pursue it. Lacking the discipline to keep up with the more than 30 hours of lectures every week, I fell behind. And if you fell behind, there was pretty much no way to catch up.

I was afraid that I would fail a class and have to retake it. I imagined what it would be like to fail a class and to be held back, to walk the hallways of the school with my head down, my shoulders cloaked in a blanket of shame, people whispering about me and wondering if I had only been admitted because of affirmative action. *Look at this guy, such a failure! Can you believe he FAILED? How dumb do you have to be? He probably didn't belong here. They probably only let him in because he was Black.* I grew more and more despondent. I took refuge in escapism. Maybe I'd take the LSAT and head to a top law school! Maybe I'd take the GMAT and get into a top business school. I'd look at their curricula and grow even more despondent—I cared even less about that stuff than I did about molecular biology and biochemistry. If I couldn't make myself give a damn about lysosomal storage diseases, I sure as hell wasn't going to enjoy reading a huge amount about torts. And what the hell were these business classes, anyway? It looked like I was going to have to do lots of the types of projects I'd always hated in school.

I had thoughts of suicide. But before I could kill myself, another student did. His name was Marwan. He was a second-generation African immigrant and I had met him on the day of my interview. That day, he had seemed so full of enthusiasm, hope, and promise. He was enrolled in the combined MD/PhD program, but after struggling for a time he had decided to drop out of the MD program to focus on his PhD. Then he decided that he wanted to be a physician after all. It was rumored that he had failed a class and was going to be held back, or even be kicked out of the PhD program. We were all shocked when we learned that he had killed himself. I hadn't been especially close to him, but I could relate to his story.

I imagined the sorrowful despair of his parents and all the sacrifices they must have made for him to know a better life than theirs. And for what? So that he might die in the prime of his life, his ambitions unachieved?

That could have been me!

I imagined my mom, disconsolate in her grief, unable to comprehend why I had killed myself. Would she blame herself? Would she ever get over it? I couldn't bear those thoughts. No, I could not and would not die. Plus, narcissist that I was, I couldn't get past the idea that people wouldn't care all that much that I was dead. Sure, they might be sad for a little bit, but then they'd quickly forget about me and move on with their lives. I tried to tell my mom about my deep depression, and how I had contemplated suicide. But such frank conversations rarely happen in our culture. It was all I could do to tell her that a student at my school had committed suicide, and how I felt sorry for his parents. She reacted much as I had expected, unable to discuss it except to tell me that she did not like hearing such things. I took this to be her way of telling me how devastated she would be if I ever did such a thing. And so, I did not share the story I had really wanted to tell—that Marwan had taken his life, and that in so doing, he had saved mine. He is the closest thing I will ever have to a Jesus.

CHAPTER 43

Hero

There is a long tradition of storytelling in Africa. When my mom was a child, people would take turns telling stories by the fire at night. She heard them so many times that she still recalls them as an adult. For whatever reason, I alone among her children got to hear bedtime stories from her as a child. They were almost always accompanied by a song in Jula. I can only remember two of these songs, unfortunately. In my case, the stories were not reinforced by years of hearing them being told and retold, so I would be hard-pressed to pass them on if I ever have children, but they remain some of my most cherished early memories.

Today, my mom no longer tells me bedtime stories, so I replicate the feeling by listening to audiobooks. I started listening to them in earnest when I was in med school. With so much studying to do, there was no opportunity to sit down with a physical book. In 2009, a year before I started med school, I'd discovered The Teaching Company. One of my favorite podcasters had mentioned them. Apparently, you could purchase audio courses and learn about topics you'd always wanted to know more about but had never quite managed to find the time to study. I fell in love. My favorite courses were in ancient Mediterranean history, linguistics, and the Middle Ages. And so, when med school started, it wasn't difficult for me to make the decision to transition to audiobooks. And it was through audiobooks that I was able to find myself a hero when I most needed one.

Alexander Hamilton had been my hero in my early years, but as he started to become a pop culture icon as a result of *Hamilton: An American Musical*, his luster started to fade for me. My understanding of the 1790s had increased, and it became easier to understand Hamilton and Jefferson within their historical context. I understood now that they represented rather than founded the governing philosophies that came to be embodied in their names. With or without Hamilton, the American North would have supported tariffs, pushed for industrialization, and slowly stirred itself in opposition to slavery. With or without Jefferson, the American political system would have democratized, and the South would have grown more dependent on and protective of slavery over the first half of the 19th century. As my understanding grew, it became harder and harder to apotheosize the one and demonize the other. I needed a new hero.

For what, after all, is a hero but a reflection of our dreams personified? A hero is hope incarnate, a momentary savior who takes us by the hand and flies us to a world well beyond our current woes, where the storm has passed, and the snows have melted, and the grass is green again. Med school was the winter of my discontent, but I did find my sun. He wasn't a scion of the House of York, but a son of America's heartland who fought on the battlefields of the Civil War. His name was Ulysses S. Grant. In time he would become president and his name, though he was a man of probity, would become a byword for the scandal and corruption in which so many of his cabinet members and associates were embroiled. But during the war, when everything seemed to be doom and gloom, his victories enabled the nation to hold on and persevere in its internecine struggle.

Ulysses S. Grant had inauspicious beginnings. He had graduated in the bottom half of his class at West Point. He did well enough during the Mexican War, but fell prey to alcoholism in the following years and was encouraged to resign from the army under threat of being fired for his drinking habit. He tried his hand at farming. He failed. He tried his hand at real estate. He failed. He applied for a job as an engineer. He failed to get the job. He seemed to be going nowhere fast. At last, he returned home to his father's leather goods store, where he worked as a clerk. The Civil War took him from this lowly position and provided him with an opportunity to shine. He proved himself to be the best strategist produced by the conflict on either side. Faced with an intractable problem, he would do what he did best—try and fail and tinker, and try and fail and tinker, and try and fail and tinker, again and again, until he found the winning formula. He was not a genius who dazzled the world with brilliant tactics. Instead, he was the epitome of American ingenuity, the man who, in a very real sense, engineered his way to ultimate victory for the Union. And it was this Union victory that made it possible for the slaves to be freed. This was a hero worth celebrating.

During med school, when I so keenly felt the full measure of my flaws, I didn't need an impeccable hero.

What I needed was a man who had known defeat and crumbled under its weight to the point that most people had written him off. What I needed was to see such a man, burned by failure, rise from his ashes and achieve success once given the opportunity. I needed this because I had written myself off as a failure. And I needed to believe that, in spite of my difficulties, I could be a good doctor if I were only given a chance to prove myself. And so Ulysses S. Grant, warts and all, with his flaws as prominent as I felt mine to be, became my greatest inspiration.

CHAPTER 44

The Tray Is Over There

I somehow managed to pass my basic science classes, but it was a close thing. I studied for Step I of the USMLE and scored around the 50th percentile. It was not a great performance, but I had escaped with my dignity intact, I thought. Now I was finally going to leave the classroom and start clinical work. I was very excited. I was going to be studying *real medicine*. I was out of the woods, at last. But I was wrong. I had traded one form of misery for another. The hours were long and the rounds were highly stressful, with people constantly asking you questions you didn't have answers to. It was no fun. I found that, except for a select few subjects, I simply didn't care enough to will myself to read everything. I studied, but I was never able to spend the hours and hours required for honors. Surgery was torture. You had to withstand god complexes, being repeatedly put down, and people being gratuitously unpleasant. Within minutes of starting my six-week clerkship, I'd already decided it wasn't the path for me.

But by this point, I was too far in and too deep in debt for quitting to be a realistic option. I felt trapped. As a first-year student, I had told myself that things would get better in second year. I had been wrong. In my second year, I had told myself that things would get better in third year.

Again, I was wrong. And as a third-year student, I told my-self things would get better in fourth year. Surprisingly, they did. Most of the hard stuff was done. There was a lot of time off for interviews for residency spots. I became noticeably happier. And this happiness persisted in resi-dency. There is an equation that summarizes my under-standing of happiness: *Happiness = reality – expectations.*

Because med school had been so emotionally taxing, I expected to be suicidal in residency, especially given the long hours in intern year. But something strange happened along the way—I became the happiest resident I knew. The work was more meaningful and I felt that I was finally learning to be a doctor. There was nothing I enjoyed more than teaching my patients about their conditions. And perhaps because I didn't take myself very seriously, I could tell that my patients enjoyed having me as their doctor.

But sometimes, it's awkward being a Black doctor. I of-ten get the impression that when people look at me, what they see first and foremost is a color. This is especially the case when my white coat isn't visible. Contact precaution gowns are a type of protective gear that we wear when we're trying to prevent the spread of certain microorgan-isms. They are usually yellow or blue, and they do a nice job of covering up whatever you're wearing, but only down to the knees if you're as tall as I am. One day, I entered the room of a patient who was on the phone. I figured I would be polite and wait a minute to give him time to finish his conversation and allow me to examine him. But, after wait-ing a bit, I realized that he was giving no sign that he would be off the phone anytime soon. And so, I said hi.

"The tray is over there," he said, pointing to his table and immediately returning to the phone. He had assumed, apparently, that I was kitchen staff. There was an awkward pause.

"Um, I'm your doctor."

He gasped in embarrassment. It was clear that the only reason he had assumed that I was from the kitchen was my complexion.

"I'm so sorry!"

"It's okay. How are you doing today?"

The rest of our interaction was uneventful, but he clearly felt mortified at what had happened. In the days that followed he was the most affable of patients and made a point of introducing me to his family and telling them how satisfied he was with my care. He was a nice guy, in truth. He'd just let himself be the victim of the kind of prejudices we are all susceptible to. I asked myself what my own assumption would have been if I had seen a Black man walk into a hospital room where I was a patient. Would I have been more likely to think *doctor* or *kitchen staff*? I couldn't be sure that my reaction would have been any different, so I gave him a pass. We all absorb negative stereotypes about people based on race. It's not that some of us are capable of racist thoughts and assumptions and some of us are not; it's that some of us choose to consciously view racism and discrimination as bad, so we override our impulses and learn to do our best to treat each other with due dignity and fairness. I know this is true because when I tell people this story, almost all of them assume that the man was White. He was, in fact, Latino.

CHAPTER 45

From African to Black

Sometimes, people ask me if I'm a feminist, and I find that I have a hard time answering. On one hand, I am decidedly not among those who hate feminism and disagree with the premise that women still have a lot of things to fight for. On the other hand, though I am in perfect sympathy with its goals, I have seen the word appropriated by misandrists enough times that I am reticent to apply it to myself. And yet, at the end of the day, movements and ideologies must be judged as being more than the sum of the excesses of their worst adherents. And so, if you restrict my options to two tribes, feminist or non-feminist, and ask me to pick a side, I will pick feminist.

Politics, at its root, is tribal, no matter what logical arguments we may advance to give an after-the-fact justification of the conclusions we have already reached. In 2016, many educated conservatives were surprised by the fact that the man who ended up winning their party's nomination was—both in his personal life and in some of the policies he had espoused over the years—the antithesis of what conservatives were supposed to stand for. They needn't have been surprised. The philosophies that many believe to constitute a party's intellectual foundation are in fact no more than a thin mantle of rationality on a thick core of tribalism. Trump won precisely because he proved to be the most adept at activating the tribal loyalties of Republican voters.

Of course, tribalism is not only a matter of party affiliation. In the US, one of the most durable and potent tribal identities is that of race, and this has never been more evident than in the stances people have taken over the various shootings of unarmed Black men that began to be more closely documented after the death of Trayvon Martin in 2012. Regardless of the circumstances of each individual case, an overall pattern can be observed in which most people consistently take the side of either the shooter or the dead man. Here again, tribalistic instincts are clothed in the garments of seemingly dispassionate arguments. But spend a few minutes in the comments section under the videos of such shootings, and you will immediately notice that what truly animates people is sympathy or antipathy towards what the dead man represents.

For those who view young Black men as thugs prone to crime, and specifically violent crime, the assumption is that if someone shoots one of them during an altercation—especially if the shooter is a police officer—they probably did so under threat of great bodily harm, and were therefore justified in killing in self-defence. All assertions to the contrary are seen as a perfect illustration of a disingenuous self-victimization. To people of this mindset, these shootings have nothing to do with race, and it is those who mention the race of the dead man who are the true racists. These people see brave police officers doing their duty and risking their lives for the protection of the public. How is it, they ask, that the protesters only seem to care about Black lives when the shooter of a Black man happens to be White?

For people who espouse this point of view, what empathy they have lies with the shooter, not with the dead man. This is most likely because they can more readily imagine themselves as a person shooting an unarmed Black man than imagine themselves as an unarmed Black man shot because he was seen to pose a mortal threat. In the years prior to the documentation of these unfortunate shootings, I had already started to distance myself from my previous views of Black American culture. By reading more about African American history and encountering highly cultured and educated African Americans in a variety of settings, I had come to see that I had judged an entire culture through the prism of my interactions with a handful of sophomoric adolescents. But with these shootings, I realized that I saw African Americans as brothers.

Given the choice of two broad tribes, one that empathized with unarmed Black men shot to death, and the other that empathized with the shooters of those men, the choice wasn't even close. I had truly wanted to believe that racism was dead when I first moved to the US, but it was impossible to live here for long without noticing that many people reflexively treat me as a threat, whether it's a woman clutching her purse in the elevator or an over-zealous store associate following me because he assumes I'm about to steal something. Likewise, the experience of having the cops called on you or of being stopped for driving while Black is nearly universal among the Black men I know. And so, it's entirely plausible to me that many people associate Blackness with criminality, even if they don't admit it to themselves. And it is also entirely plausible that, during an altercation, this bias they have against men of African descent would make them perceive a mortal threat where none exists and act accordingly. So, when I watch a video of an unarmed Black man shot without reason, what I see is someone *like me* being shot. And that is how I know that I am no longer merely an African living in America, but that I have become Black.

CHAPTER 46

Visiting Vancouver

Imagine a world devoid of anti-Black racism, where people aren't mistreated for being Black, and where they aren't treated differently from other people. Instead, your skin complexion is treated as just as inconsequential a facet of who you are as your eye color. Would there be any race consciousness in such a world? Would people who share the same complexion feel any tribal affiliation or any special affinity towards one another? I got a chance to find out the answer to these questions when I traveled to Vancouver, British Columbia, Canada, where Black people comprise only 1% of the population.

For the first half of my life, I was an African living in Africa, where my race was naturally the least remarkable of my features. But I've lived in the US for most of my life now, and here, it is undeniable that being Black is definitely *a thing*. It sets you apart, and not necessarily in a positive way. You are a minority. And even if you try to pretend that race doesn't exist, or is irrelevant, society will sooner or later remind you that you are Black, and that everything else is a minor detail. If this is at first disconcerting, it feels perversely normal after a while. It is just what it is. In such an environment, there's a strong consciousness of being Black, whether you live in a place with a large Black population such as Atlanta, or a place like Portland, Oregon, where about 6% of the population is Black. I was sitting at a French-style cafe in Portland in June 2018 when a Black man entered. Immediately he took a seat next to mine. We gave each other the nod and started talking. We were the only two Black people in the place. He was a physical therapist, about 50 years old, who had grown up in the area, and he told the story of how his neighborhood had changed over the decades. He told me about growing up Black in Portland in the '70s, an experience that, for all of the vaunted liberalism of the city, sounded no more fun than that of growing up in places reputed to be more racist. In Portland as elsewhere, to be a young Black man was to be a suspicious other.

This is what it means to be Black in America: to be able to discuss such stories within a few minutes of meeting a stranger, and to be confident that they will be able to relate. The flip side of racial otherness is that you come to see every other member of your race as a brother. This is especially true when you're in a place where Blacks are a small minority. Every time you see another Black person, you give each other a sign of acknowledgment. *I see you over there, fellow Black person, fellow passenger in this slow ride towards justice and equality, fellow fighter in the struggle. I see you. And I salute you.* My experience in Vancouver was the exact opposite. Blackness, it turned out, was decidedly not *a thing* there. I searched the eyes of the Black people I encountered for a sign, a token of acknowledgment, a special greeting, anything, but all in vain. I'd come to expect it, to see it as normal, living in the US.

But there was nothing. Not a smile, not a nod, not even a second glance. I was not a fellow Black person to them; I was a perfect stranger, and an odd one at that. As I waited for a sign of acknowledgment that never came, the only message I could read in their eyes was a series of questions: *Why is this fellow looking at me like that? Is he going to get out of my way? Hello! Can I help you?* For the first time in half my life, I did not feel Black. I could just be me, just another person who merely happened to be chocolate-hued. It was truly liberating to be a human rather than a Black human, for a change. And yet, much as I celebrated this newfound freedom, I realized that I had come to enjoy the feeling that other Blacks constituted a shield and a community for me. In this way, too, I had become a Black American.

CHAPTER 47

A Rewarding Field

I'm a physiatrist, a specialist in physical medicine and rehabilitation. It's a bit of a mouthful, and for that reason, it's usually abbreviated as PM&R. I had only the vaguest idea that this field existed when I started med school. I'm highly introverted and I need a lot of time alone, so I was convinced that I would be interested in radiology. But there were three things that steered me away from that field. The first of these was that, while I loved the fact that radiologists got a lot of time off and were very well paid, I did not actually like radiology itself. The second reason was that with my grades and test scores, while it wouldn't be impossible for me to enter the field, I would certainly not have been considered a top-tier applicant. Finally, I was very concerned that I would miss something really important that later turned out to be something serious like a cancer. I could not live with that kind of anxiety.

So much for radiology, then. But it was easier for me to decide what I didn't want to do than what I wanted to pursue. My girlfriend told me that she thought the rotation on which I had been happiest was my outpatient internal medicine one. It was hard for me to disagree with her. I really did love my time on that rotation. It was like being a family doctor, but without pediatrics and obstetrics, which I very much did not want to do. But there was no such thing as an outpatient internal medicine residency. I would have to learn the entire field, including intensive care, which seemed, well, intensive. The very idea of doing a 24-hour shift in the ICU filled me with dread. This was never going to work, I decided.

I then realized that by far my favorite thing to do was the neurological physical exam. It was like solving an electrical puzzle and trying to figure out where a wire was damaged. It was fun! I could let out my inner toddler as I had people copy my facial expressions, or call people haters for telling me that my reflex hammer didn't make me look like Thor, or even make funny sounds as I checked their reflexes. Beyond this, I genuinely liked reading about the pathology of stroke and acquired demyelinating neuropathies. But as I looked at program after program, I could not get over the fact that the hours of training were very long. Perhaps, if I had lived in Europe, where work-hour restrictions for doctors in training had been embraced, I would have become a neurologist. But the idea of consistently working 70 or more hours per week was a deterrent. Yet again, I would have to find something else.

Towards the middle of my third year of med school, I became friends with Kathleen, whom I creatively nick-named Blondie because of the color of her hair. She was one of the few people with whom I could honestly discuss the issue of work-life balance without feeling I was imme-diately being seen as lazy. We were type B personalities in a type A world. She thought she had found the holy grail in PM&R. I was skeptical. I had never once seriously considered it, but I decided to keep it in mind. By that point, I was also considering Emergency Medicine, so I scheduled a PM&R rotation right after my EM rotation. Very quickly, I realized that while I liked the schedule of EM, I did not actually like the work, and I had the wrong kind of personality for it. Everyone else seemed to be much more hardcore than I was.

I went to my PM&R rotation not expecting much. But by the end of the first day, I knew I had found my field. When people ask you why or how you chose a certain field, the temptation is to give them some logical explanation. I can erect an edifice of logical clauses for why I pursued this path, but logic was not why I chose my field. It was an emotional decision, truth be told. I liked the atmosphere. I liked the relaxed personalities of the physicians I was working with. I liked the fact that with a small intervention like a steroid injection, I could make a meaningful difference in quality of life for people suffering from a variety of debilitating or simply irritating ailments. It was definitely the right choice for me. Still, it's a bit hard to explain what it is exactly that I do.

So, you're a physical therapist?

Well, no. I work with physical therapists, and physical therapy is something I often prescribe, but I am a physician.

So, you're a sports medicine doc?

Well, not quite, but sometimes, maybe? I definitely see a lot of people with sports-type injuries.

So, what do you do, again?

I'm a physician of function. That's the most concise way I can explain it. I take people who have some measure of decline in their function, such as walking, playing sports, dressing, driving, balancing their checkbook, or emptying their bowel or bladder, and I help them maximize their level of function. Generally, the patients I work with have some kind of neurological or musculoskeletal disorder—stroke, traumatic brain injury, spinal cord injury, various flavors of back pain, carpal tunnel syndrome, tennis elbow, and the like. Sometimes I'm managing the medication regimen of a patient with spasticity from a stroke or spinal cord injury that is causing them to have a hard time walking or getting in and out of bed. Sometimes I'm doing steroid injections in the knees or shoulders of patients with arthritis. Sometimes, I'm an electromyographer and I diagnose people with nerve or muscle disease. Sometimes I give guidance to people on returning to play or work after they've had a concussion or a more severe traumatic brain injury. Other times, I'm working with amputees to help fit them with a proper prosthetic device. Overall, it's a pretty rewarding field.

CHAPTER 48

The End of the War

Amid mutual recriminations and the breakdown of trust between all parties, Ivory Coast remained partitioned in the years following the rebellion. The rebels, renamed the New Forces, were happy to keep control of half the country, together with the wealth flowing from its agricultural and mineral resources. Gbagbo, in turn, was happy to preside over the richer half of the country. And so, 2005 came and went without an election. The president remained in office, and stated that the refusal of the rebels to disarm proved that the conditions didn't exist for a credible national election.

Between 2003 and 2010, many agreements were broken by both sides. But it was finally agreed that elections would take place in 2010, and all major candidates were allowed to participate. In the first round, the top two contenders were Gbagbo and Ouattara, who received 38% and 32% of the vote respectively. Since no one obtained 50% of the vote, a runoff election took place. Both sides heavily courted Bédié, who had received 25% of the first-round vote. The question for the second round was which of the other candidates Bédié's supporters hated more. Bédié had made an alliance with Ouattara—they had agreed before the election to support each other, should one fail to qualify for the second round. So, Bédié called on his supporters to vote for Ouattara. But many of these supporters were from the Akan group, and Christian. It was unclear how willing they would be to vote for the Muslim Ouattara.

As the results from the second round of voting were tabulated, it became apparent that Ouattara was winning, thanks to massive support in the northern half of the country. Voting behaviour is very tribalistic in Africa. The same patterns from the first round were repeated, but the alliance between Bédié and Ouattara held and made a difference. Before the results were released, the president's supporters objected. On national TV, one of the president's supporters ripped the papers out of the hands of the president of the National Electoral Commission as he was about to announce the results. This was not a good sign.

Nevertheless—over the objections of Gbagbo and under the protection of the UN—the president of the Electoral Commission managed to announce that Ouattara had won the election. Now the UN was added to the list of the president's enemies, and his supporters were convinced that there was a massive international conspiracy to rob them of their victory. This was fueled by the fact that the announcement of the results took place at the hotel where Ouattara was staying under UN protection. To the president's supporters, this looked like evidence of a plot. To everyone else, it merely looked like the results had been announced there because that was where the UN troops were stationed, and the man making the announcement had well-founded reasons to fear for his safety.

At this point, friends of the president in the international community begged him to acknowledge defeat and step down. But he refused, and instead doubled down. He declared results in some northern regions invalid, citing fraud but providing no more evidence than the lopsided margins of victory his opponent had received there. He declared the results in more and more northern regions as void until he could safely claim a majority. Northerners, of course, were not going to accept this without a fight, and civil war quickly resumed. In rapid succession, city after city fell to the New Forces. For the first time, it appeared that there might be a prolonged battle in the streets of Abidjan, where the loyalist forces had reinforced their positions over the years. Having swept aside everything in their wake on the road to Abidjan, the rebels found that they were unable to dislodge Gbagbo from the fortified presidential compound.

Months had now passed since the election, and the French again made the decision to intervene. They bombarded key positions and allowed the rebel forces to storm into the presidential palace. Gbagbo and his entourage were captured. It was the end of the civil war, at last. But for many across Africa, Gbagbo was a hero, a brave leader who had stood up to the forces of European neocolonialism. I will never look at that man and see a hero, but there is a measure of truth to the idea that this French intervention was not purely altruistic. As president, Ouattara has been exceedingly friendly towards French business interests. And yet, much as I deplore neocolonialism, I cannot be blind to the fact that French intervention validated the results of the elections. And the country has done well economically since then, although the high rates of growth have not allowed most of the population to keep up with the pace of inflation.

Despite the new president's reputation as a man of probity, by the time he reached power, he had accumulated too many political debts that needed to be repaid, and his regime proved to be no less corrupt than those of his predecessors. Those of us who had expectantly waited for a new regime of governmental honesty and efficiency were sorely disappointed. Corruption was still a useful tool of governance, and the judiciary was much too impotent for meaningful change to occur. Instead, the tribalism of the north replaced the tribalism of the south, and venality still reigns in Abidjan. There are some who see Ouattara's accession to the presidency as the triumph of democracy over tyranny. But what actually triumphed was the force of arms, and French arms at that. This is a lesson that was lost on none of the main characters in the long drama of Ivorian politics. Whatever idealists may choose to believe, whatever pageantry is used to disguise it after the fact, and whatever poetry is associated with professions of belief in the rule of law, the stark reality is that political power continues to come out of the barrel of a gun.

The other lesson provided by this depressing story is that it pays to be on the winning side. Although war crimes and atrocities were committed by both sides, the overwhelming majority of people punished for them were on Gbagbo's side. I was not one of his supporters, but I will freely acknowledge that it was a case of victor's justice. And this is all the more deplorable because it is unlikely that the many wounds created by the conflict will heal anytime soon. For my own part, as soon as it became clear to me that the new president would not be the anti-corruption reformer I had hoped for, I lost interest in Ivorian politics. I have not looked back. I will never vote in any Ivorian election. I am now an American who just happens to have lived the first half of his life in Ivory Coast.

CHAPTER 49

Home

Seventeen years after my departure, I finally visited Ivory Coast again. Friends and acquaintances congratulated me even before I left. "Oh, you're going to visit your country? That must be so exciting!" But I was not excited. I was apprehensive, contemplating how much both the country and I had changed in divergent directions, and wondering whether I would be able to fit in. Would I feel that I was in my country? Or would I instead feel that I was a foreigner who just happened to speak French with the local accent? I suspected it would be the latter, and as the day of departure approached, my apprehension grew.

I had asked my mom to come with me to help prevent me from committing too many cultural faux pas. As we sat in the airport on the night of our departure, an event occurred that confirmed my suspicions. A woman in her 40s or early 50s was standing by us. She had apparently been looking at me for a while with some dissatisfaction before she spoke, and it was only when she repeated what she had said that I realized her words had been addressed to me. By this time she was sitting next to me. I looked up from my phone, smiled at her, and politely told her that I did not speak Jula. She seemed taken aback and didn't offer to translate what she had said. A few minutes later, she was gone, and my mom asked me whether I had understood what the woman had said. I told her that I had not.

Apparently, she had told me—twice—something to the effect of "Our young Jula men today no longer rise to offer their seat to an older woman, isn't that right?" She had meant to shame me into giving up my seat for her! Her plan had obviously failed, leaving me more confused than ashamed, but I could not help but feel annoyed. The American in me could not believe that she would dare to tell me when and to whom I should offer my seat. But this was normal behavior in my home culture—a culture that was evidently no longer mine.

The 10-hour flight in coach was uncomfortable, but as we neared landing and I saw the familiar light-blue waters of the Ebrie Lagoon—probably Abidjan's most recognizable natural landmark—I found myself tearing up. I had apparently missed this country more than I had realized. I soon realized that in traveling I had shed my exoticism—everyone around me was an African who spoke French with the characteristic intonations and expressions of Ivory Coast. I felt silly for having thought that I no longer belonged there. I was home.

But my reverie abruptly ended when the border agent solicited money from me, and all of a sudden, I felt like a foreigner again. I sighed internally and handed her the lone $10 bill remaining in my wallet, much to her apparent satisfaction. Then I learned that only one of my two suitcases had arrived with me. The missing bag was my larger suitcase, which I had purchased only the day before my departure. I had been pretty satisfied with it, but now it was nowhere to be found. At lost and found, I was told that either my suitcase hadn't been loaded in Newark, or it had been mistakenly flown to Addis Ababa, or it had been taken by another passenger. I was told that the airline would call me in three days, when things had been sorted out. At this, I frowned, expecting not to see it again.

I had thankfully kept in my carry-on my laptops and the tablets I had brought as gifts, but this was still irksome. There was nothing valuable in the missing suitcase, which contained only clothes and toiletries. But I was annoyed that I would now have to stop somewhere to buy such things as underwear and toothpaste. It was a bit of a first-world problem in a third-world country, but it was still a problem. I had not yet shed my irritation when, for the first time since my departure from Ivory Coast half a lifetime ago, I saw my sister Sally.

Sally is our French rendering of Salimata, my maternal grandmother's name and a Jula rendering of the Arabic name Salima. Sally is six years my elder, and growing up, I thought she was the meanest girl in the world. As a child, she had once slapped me so hard that she left a handprint on my cheek, and then laughed at me for having a handprint on my cheek. She was tyrannical. But there was no animosity between us as adults. Still, happy as I was to see her again, our reunion was not very emotional. In the many years since I had left, we had kept in touch less and less frequently, at first because it was inconvenient and expensive, but in the end because we had simply lost the habit. We caught up and traded old stories on our way to the apartment she had reserved for me and my mom.

We arrived at the place to find that it had two problems. The first was that no one knew the Wi-Fi password. I was not happy about it, but felt that I could wait until the morning. The second problem wasn't as easily shrugged off. Not only were there cockroaches in the sink and on the kitchen floor, but the fridge had been unplugged, and they had taken to living in there, too. That did it. This place was definitely not going to work. But events took a brighter turn when my 14-year-old nephew arrived. He was named after me, and I had seen many pictures of him since his birth in 2004, but he had not existed when I left. I hugged him so tightly that we almost fell. He must have wondered who this crazy uncle who was trying to kill him moments after meeting him was. But his opinion of me appeared to take a sharp turn for the positive when I handed him the laptop I'd brought for him. Now it was his turn to bear hug me with all the force he could muster, and we laughed and laughed and laughed.

CHAPTER 50

Uncle

It had been 17 years since I had last set foot in Abidjan, and I had the feeling that if I waited another 17 years, all of my uncles and aunts would be dead by the time of my next visit. By far my favorite part of being there was meeting the youngest members of my family. Aside from my nephew Habib, there were my brother Kader's three children. Kader is 12 years older than me, and I mention him so infrequently that people are often surprised to hear that I have a brother. And yet, I have never had occasion to complain about him. It's simply that, after many years apart, and many missed phone calls in both directions, we lost the habit of being brothers. Now, it amused me that he looked so much older than I remembered him. It's one thing to know that your brother is no longer the 27-year-old you left behind, but it's quite another to see him face-to-face as a middle-aged man.

We met twice during my week-long stay, and our conversations mostly revolved around the fate of the country and the mostly unfulfilled hopes that had followed the end of the war. Whereas I saw mostly cultural and structural factors that could be fixed in time, with the development of an independent judiciary and a commitment to government for the people, he felt comfortable with a rather impolitic line of inquiry. He entertained the notion that there was perhaps a genetic defect inherent to the African psyche that accounted for so much mismanagement and poor governance on the continent. He added that he was not saying that this was necessarily the case, but that he merely thought that question was worth asking. I had heard variations of this theme from many other educated Africans over the years, so I wasn't taken aback. Still, I had been away too long for this view to be congenial to me, and I argued that it was probably more a problem of nurture than of nature.

Before this trip to Ivory Coast, I knew that Kader had three kids, but I could only name two of them and hadn't seen pictures of any of them. Now, I met them at my Uncle Karim's house. The oldest was at this time a 10-year-old boy named Ishan. Upon being introduced to me, he gave me one look, nodded, and moved on with the rest of his day. To him, I was just another stranger, allegedly his father's younger brother, who happened to have the same name as his cousin Habib. He couldn't have cared less, and I couldn't blame him. Ishan had a 7-year-old sister, Jamila, who looked like a photocopy of her mother, whom I had seen pictures of but had never met. The youngest child was a girl named Mounira, a toddler who loved cake and who demanded to have Happy Birthday sung to her every time one was brought out.

On my second visit to their home, I found Ishan and Jamila playing a video game. It was FIFA 16, and they seemed to be enjoying themselves. I asked them if I could play the winner, and they agreed. Jamila won and she looked at me with an expectation of easy victory painted all over her face. I suppressed a smile as they guided me through the basic commands. What these kids had no way of knowing is that, though I hadn't played FIFA in at least three years, I had probably spent more hours of my life playing the various iterations of this one game since 1995 than either of them had spent playing video games. So, when the game started, the first thing Jamila noticed was that she was having a hard time even touching the ball. Ishan impatiently took over from her. He couldn't believe that she was having a hard time playing against a beginner. Shortly afterwards, I scored. I could see that he thought this was probably a fluke, and that my being ahead was something he would rectify very soon. But then I used a feint, tricking his goalie and scoring a second goal.

Hey, Uncle, how did you do that? Wait a minute! It looks like this uncle can play. I think this uncle has played before.

Now it was Jamila's turn to be impatient. She snatched the controller back from her brother. At least when she had been playing, I hadn't been able to score. Moments later, I scored my third goal, laughing all the while, and eventually explaining that I had been playing these games almost all my life. I left them with a little gift before I left. I think they were appeased.

CHAPTER 51

Defective

In August of 2018, I fell in love with a girl who spanked me. I was visiting my cousin Kevin, who lives in France. He is the son of my Uncle Karim, one of my father's younger brothers. In my early teenage years, and until the day I left Ivory Coast, we had been almost inseparable, and we continued to keep in touch through the years. Kevin had two daughters, the youngest of whom was not quite three years old. Her name was Lili. She was fierce, energetic, and exceedingly opinionated. Every aquatic animal was a dolphin. And if you told her that what she was looking at was actually a shark, she would correct you.

Non! Dauphin!

Likewise, every body of water, whether it was the sea or a lake or a stream, was the Loire. And she would keep on correcting you until, suitably beaten into submission, you at last admitted that she was right. Sometimes when you disagreed, she would ask if you wanted to be spanked.

Tu veux une fessée?

She asked me this after I dared to disagree with her. And before I realized what was happening, she was running towards me and spanking me! I laughed so hard that I fell into the couch, whereupon she continued spanking me. I had no energy left to fight her off.

Lili and I had a game in which we would wrinkle our noses, growl at each other, then get close and share an Eskimo kiss. The night before I left, I tucked her into bed. I tried to explain that I was leaving France for good. She could not grasp what I was saying. But, uncharacteristically, she reached over and gave me a peck on the lips. My heart melted, knowing that the next time I saw her, she would have forgotten about me.

If I fall so easily in love with the children of others, it is because I can't have children of my own, not without in vitro fertilization, in any case. I first suspected it might be the case when I learned as a 25-year-old medical student that I had a varicocele. This is an enlargement of the scrotal veins that results in an alteration of blood flow and testicular temperatures. Because there is a known association with male infertility, I started bracing myself for the idea that I might not be able to have children. Later, I wanted to know for sure, and so at 32, I underwent a semen analysis. Intellectualization has always been my favorite coping mechanism—it allows me to pretend to have a detachment and maintain my equanimity. It did not quite work this time.

Only 2% of the sperm in my sample were viable, and none of them were motile. The low-end normal figures are 58% viability and 40% motility. Apparently, I'm not just infertile; I am *very* infertile. I always underestimate the power of my emotions. I see this as a relic of my adolescence, when I fell in love with enlightenment thinking and the near deification of the concept of reason. It was reason that separated humans from animals, and the greatest virtue was the ability to use reason to conquer one's passions. I no longer subscribe to those views, but habits of the mind are hard to change. After developing a self-image of myself as a thinking man, it's hard for me not to expect that, whether I am going through a breakup or learning that I am infertile, I will simply accept the new reality and move on with the rest of my life. I am always surprised when my emotions disregard my own theories of who and what I am and assert themselves.

This time was no different. I was incredulous at finding myself gripped by a profound sadness. I felt defective, like some sentient machine learning that it had been shipped with a malfunctioning part. I thought of surgery but quickly rejected the idea. This was not what I wanted. Part of my surprise was that in the preceding two years, I had come around to the idea that maybe I did not want children after all. But it was one thing to consciously make the decision for oneself, having weighed the pluses and minuses, and quite another to have the choice taken away from me. I thought of adoption, but soon realized that it wasn't the idea of not being able to raise children that saddened me. It was the idea of not being able to father kids. Although my intellect told me that any child I raised would be mine regardless of whether they shared my genetic material, it did nothing to pull me out of my despondency. I thought of the journal I had spent eight years writing to my unborn children. I thought of all the money I had spent on birth control and laughed at myself. I thought of the rising cost of college and smiled. There, at least, was a silver lining. But soon enough I was sad again. I thought of telling my parents, then quickly rejected the idea. Maybe someday I would, but right now, I didn't want to tell them. They would make a huge fuss about it. I wanted the space and time to grieve in my own way, without having to deal with their grief at the idea that they would not have grandchildren by me.

CHAPTER 52

The Scent of Lemongrass

I like the scent of lemongrass. For me it will always remain the scent of childhood and innocence, of the tender caresses of a tropical sun, and of the joy of insouciance. Lemongrass is the perfume of games of hide-and-seek, of the welcoming arms of my mother, and of a life lived close to siblings and long-lost friends. It is the aroma of fried plantains at 4 o'clock in the afternoon, of croissants and pains-aux-raisins on Sunday mornings, and of whole days spent playing video games. In short, it is the scent of nostalgia, of that long-gone universe where I was a child, and everyone was chocolate-hued and French-speaking, and every woman I met told me how cute my dimples were, and the wealth was still flowing, and the civil war lay far in the future. Lemongrass is my time-traveling machine. It is the lips of my mother on my forehead and cheeks. It is my lullaby. It is my comfort. It is pure, distilled, and unadulterated joy.

But sometimes, after spending hours in a room while my aromatherapy diffuser spreads this bewitching scent into every corner, I realize that I can no longer smell it. It is only when I return after leaving the room for a while that I can perceive it again. It is similar with growing up in a country and leaving for a while. There were things that I did not perceive, because they were the norm and I knew nothing else. But after a prolonged absence, what was once home became foreign to my sensibilities. All of a sudden, I was very conscious that I had grown up in a third-world nation. Only, unlike the scent of lemongrass, which was pleasing, most of what I saw in this former land of mine made me frown. The lack of sidewalks, the vendors occupying half the streets, the excessive and suffocating pollution, the chaotic and aggressive driving culture in which there was no such thing as a right of way. Everything was a turnoff.

Many Ivorians were proud of the improvements that had been made in the city landscape. But while it was undeniable that there had been lots of construction projects in the years of my absence, what was apparent to me was how far the country had to go. Officially, Ivory Coast has a traffic code. But, corruption being what it is, people who don't study are still issued a driver's license if they are willing to pay the right bribe to the right person. Over time, more and more people have taken this route and today the bribe is an obligation—no matter how well you know the code, some reason will be found to fail you if you don't pay. Logically, people have stopped studying. Why bother studying if you're going to be given a license anyway? So now we have a situation where the vast majority of drivers have never studied anything about the driving code, which has for all practical purposes stopped existing. This is how we find ourselves in an environment where people don't have a notion that there is such a thing as a right of way. Here, driving courtesy is punished. If you want to make a left turn, the usual practice is to throw your car in the way of oncoming traffic and dare the other driver to hit you. The only thing drivers respect with any measure of consistency are red lights. Stop signs are routinely ignored. And, when arriving at a traffic circle, rather than waiting for already engaged drivers to pass, most people will speed as much as possible in an attempt to overtake and block oncoming vehicles.

This chaotic driving culture, with its general disregard for rules and regulations or any sort, is a sad metaphor for the organization of Ivorian society. There are almost no rules that can't be circumvented with money. If you don't want to study for your driver's license, you bribe someone. If your vehicle is polluting too much, but you want to continue driving it, you bribe someone. If you don't want to pay the taxes you owe, you bribe someone. If you want to be awarded a government contract, you bribe someone. And if you don't want to throw away your water bottle while going through airport security, you bribe someone. It would be difficult, even for a reform-minded president, to change any of this. For a long time, I saw the crisis of governance as a problem of a parasitic political class siphoning off resources that would better be utilized to improve the living conditions of the masses. This picture was not entirely wrong, but it was incomplete. Corruption is not merely a tool of the elite. It is also an integral part of the culture, permeating transactions in both the private and public system. Corruption still reigns because the status quo benefits a large number of people, even if it is to the detriment of society as a whole.

As I thought of this, I came to the uncomfortable realization that I had become, in all but the most superficial of ways, thoroughly estranged from the land of my birth. I spoke with the local accent, had a fondness for some of the local foods, and wore shirts embroidered with local motifs, but I was for all practical purposes a foreigner in the land of my birth. When I returned to the US, I caught myself feeling relieved and elated at finally being back in my own country. Up to that point, I had meant Ivory Coast whenever I mentioned "my country." But now, it was clear to me for the first time just how much of an American I had become.

Conclusion

The morning after graduation, in June 2018, I had the strange sensation that everything I had worked for had been accomplished. Now what? Up to then, there had always been an obvious next step towards the next milestone—graduation from nursing school, taking med school pre-reqs, taking the MCAT, graduating from med school, matching into a residency program, graduating from residency, and finding a job. But now all of these had been done, and there was no blueprint, no hard endpoint, no footsteps to follow. There was just an inscrutable future towards which I looked in vain for some guidance. I had no wife, no children, no family to care for. I was perfectly free. But there was paralysis in this freedom, and I found myself strangely apprehensive, now that I had attained the goals I had worked so hard to reach.

With the future uncertain, I looked back at the past, and the improbable journey that led me to where I am now. To everyone else, I looked like a success story. I had, after all, come from what Trump called a shithole country, unable to speak the language of my host nation, and had found academic success and respectability after years of hard work. But I was conscious of all my failings, of the many moments of deep depression along the way, of the times when the only thing that prevented me from quitting was that I had no viable escape. I was also aware that there had been many instances in which timely assistance from someone who believed in me allowed me to succeed. It was impossible for me to see in my story a classic tale of rags to riches in which the protagonist, faced with seemingly insurmountable odds, triumphs by dint of hard work and determination.

What, then, is my story? It is a tale of immigration, a story as old as the idea of America itself, but with the added modern flavor of living under the threat of deportation. It is a tale of a flawed and not all that special protagonist seeing his hopes and dreams fulfilled. It is the tale of a young African who—after a long but necessarily incomplete process of assimilation into the West—gradually becomes an American, and is more at ease in his adoptive country than anywhere else in the world. And lastly, it is an illustration of all the factors that it takes to allow a young African to succeed in modern America. I flatter myself that it was a story worth telling.

Also from Thorntree Press

Love's Not Color Blind: Race and Representation in Polyamorous and Other Alternative Communities
Kevin A. Patterson, with a foreword by Ruby Bouie Johnson

"Kevin does amazing work both centering the voices of people of color and educating white folks on privilege. His words will positively influence polyamorous communities for years to come."
— Rebecca Hiles, The Frisky Fairy

This Heart Holds Many: My Life as the Nonbinary Millennial Child of a Polyamorous Family
Koe Creation, with a foreword by Dr. Elisabeth Sheff

"Having a firsthand account by someone who lived and loved and learned in a polyamorous household is invaluable to any of us who raise children in the same environment."
— Kevin A. Patterson, curator of Poly Role Models and author of *Love's Not Color Blind*

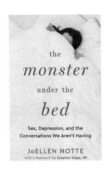

The Monster Under the Bed: Sex, Depression, and the Conversations We Aren't Having

JoEllen Notte, with a foreword by Stephen Biggs, RP

"JoEllen dared to speak about a topic no one else would and has changed the way we think about sex and depression. Her work is, quite simply, invaluable."
— Tristan Taormino, sex educator, host of Sex Out Loud Radio, and author of *Opening Up*

Black Iron

Franklin Veaux and Eve Rickert

"This is a delightful and promising steampunk adventure."
— Publishers Weekly

A Whore's Manifesto: An Anthology of Writing and Artwork by Sex Workers

Edited by Kay Kassirer, with a foreword by Clementine Von Radics

"This book evolves sex work authored literature as we know it."
— Amber Dawn, author of *How Poetry Saved My Life: A Hustler's Memoir*

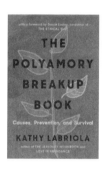

The Polyamory Breakup Book: Causes, Prevention, and Survival

Kathy Labriola, with a foreword by Dossie Easton

"Mandatory reading for those considering an adventure into the world of consensual non-monogamy."
— Ken Haslam, MD, founder of the Ken Haslam Polyamory Archives, the Kinsey Institute, Indiana University

Disrupting the Bystander: When #metoo Happens Among Friends

A.V. Flox, with a foreword by Feminista Jones

"If you've ever felt helpless in the face of someone else's discomfort or pain, this book will teach you how to show up and stand up."
— Laszlo Bock, CEO of Humu and author of *Work Rules! Insights from Inside Google to Transform How You Live and Lead*

Ask: Building Consent Culture

Edited by Kitty Stryker, with a foreword by Laurie Penny

"There are certain conversations that deepen how you think; positively impact how you act; expand your view and understanding of the world, and forever alter how you approach it. This book is full of them. Make room for it—then spread the word."
— Alix Fox, journalist, sex educator and ambassador for the Brook sexual wellbeing charity